"Tiny Baby Girl Found in Woods"

A Memoir

Mary Ellen Cordell Donat
with
Mary Ellen Test Suey

from personal recollections of the compelling true story

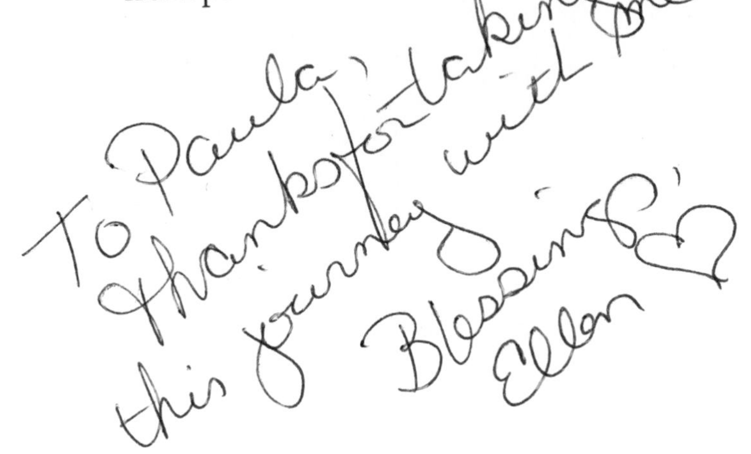

Cover art by Tom Donat

Print and ebook formatting by Steven W. Booth, GeniusBookServices.com

Dedication

For Marga and Merwin Test
and
Betty and Corky Cordell

followers of Christ who raised their daughters
to know and love the Lord

Acknowledgments

First and foremost, we give honor and glory to The Triune God: God the Father, God the Son and God the Holy Spirit. We are thankful for His love, mercy, grace, and guidance. Most of all, we are grateful that He has provided for everyone victory over sin and death. There is one Truth: Jesus Christ lived, died, was buried, and was resurrected in three days so that all who believe have eternal life in His presence. It is our hope that readers will accept His free gift.

Heartfelt gratitude is extended to the following friends and family who contributed to this memoir in a myriad of ways, including sharing professional knowledge, personal stories, photographs, memories, and most important, selflessly giving us the encouragement to write this memoir (in alphabetical order following our parents and husbands):

- **Merwin and Marga Test**, Ellen's late parents, who lovingly adopted and raised her;

- **Edward "Corky" and Betty Cordell**, Mary Ellen's late parents, who never forgot the tiny abandoned baby, and kept Rose Wayne's story alive with their daughter through the decades;
- **Bob Suey,** Ellen's husband, whom Ellen says patiently listened to hours of her chatter on this subject;
- **Tom Donat**, Mary Ellen's husband, who spent countless hours sacrificing and encouraging as Mary Ellen researched and wrote (he also provided the cover art);
- **Richard Benner**, who shared memories, stories and photos of his late father and mother, **Julian and Meta Jane Benner**;
- **Peggy Branstrator**, former Indiana University East science professor, who explained in detail valuable information concerning parasites mentioned in this memoir;
- **John Catey**, former Wayne County sheriff, who relayed details of his 2013 search for the grown Roseann Wayne;
- **Bill Engle**, former Palladium-Item journalist, who graciously gave permission to reprint his articles in this memoir;
- The late **Suzi Fryman**, who provided written details about her interest in and research concerning the search for Roseann Wayne;
- **Janet Hart Heinicke**, the daughter of the late Wayne County Department of Welfare case worker **Mary Hart**, who provided information about her mother and a photograph of her;

- **Gary Kitchel**, who described the character and sites of 1955 Boston, Indiana;
- **Joyce Melling**, who described baby Rose Wayne's appearance and visit to the Wayne County jail the day of her adoption;
- **Debra Pierce Porter**, who for years encouraged Ellen to tell her story;
- **Kevin and Gina Shendler**, Ellen's cousin and his wife, who helped with the 2014 reunion reception;
- **Tammy Shendler**, Search Angel and Ellen's cousin-in-law, who was instrumental in helping Ellen discover her identity, relayed memories concerning the search, and kindly shared her own story with Mary Ellen.

Prologue

Maybe she was just scared. Fear will do that. Make her take an infant still warm and wet from the womb, yank the pinking shears across the tentacle of its umbilical cord and, without knotting the graying cable, grab a soiled towel from the rack over the porcelain tub to loosely cover the baby girl's quivering torso. Fear of having her life, reputation, and future potential suddenly as stained as that tainted towel will cause her to at last clumsily wrap the trademarked terry cloth around the squealing babe writhing on the cold tiles of the bloody floor.

Then leave her there for a day or more.

Or maybe that venal fear makes her pick up the scarlet bundle and carry it immediately to a 1955 Cadillac Eldorado, or perhaps it was a 1938 Ford pick-up, and drive the newborn a half hour from home, windshield wipers barely keeping the glass clear to see rain-soaked cornfields along a solitary Indiana road. Just maybe she could make out stands of oak and walnut trees becoming dense woods, thick weeds hiding rough trunks. That's the place, her fear says.

Days or hours after pulling the little girl from between her legs, alone in the middle of the night, wedged between the commode and claw-foot tub, fear gives her the strength to lean over the drooping barbed wire fence to drop the bundle heavily to the soggy ground. Through clouds of breath she can see that the baby is satisfactorily hidden in the tall, sodden weeds beside the fencepost. Rain beats tat-a-tat in an ever increasing crescendo identical to her terrible heartbeats.

She quickly walks away, pulling her soaked coat closer against chill and fear.

So, maybe she was selfish and scared.

Or maybe she was heartbroken. Young and unmarried, she delivered the evidence of sin that had the power to shame entire families in unforgiving 1955. Did she lie hopelessly devastated on a blood-soaked mattress that frosty autumn night, begging the man who'd fathered the child to return the baby girl he'd taken from her at the child's first cry?

Had she loved the life that had grown in her belly, yearned to hold her? Maybe she hoped to keep her. Or thought the father would realize love for the baby, too, and they'd invent a lie. Perhaps her mind raced as she, together with someone as equally afraid and self-centered, discussed what might be done with this inconvenient, dark interruption in the bright light of their youth and promise.

If she was thinking anything in her personal grief and pain, though, she was probably not thinking at that moment that the baby would be left to surely die in frigid, dark, sodden woods.

For that's the only certainty. The days-old baby, its umbilical cord coagulated by thick blood and stuck to a worn and tattered hotel towel, was dropped by a fence post near the edge of dense woods along a solitary country road. No doorstep or gas station lavatory, no firehouse mailbox or hospital front stoop.

This baby was meant to die.

Like the men who threw Joseph into the pit, whoever left this infant in that thicket of weeds meant it for evil. But God used it for good.

Foreword

The following account of the story of a tiny baby abandoned in dank, deserted woods is a memoir written as a narrative. Ellen Suey, the infant who'd been left to die, recalls incidents from her childhood, tells how she discovered the details of her terrible infancy, relates trials and heartbreak of adulthood, and reflects on how she has been inspired through her unique circumstances.

This memoir also includes memories and experiences of the daughter of the sheriff who yearned to adopt the abandoned baby. Her contribution to this memoir includes her father's numerous recountings of the actual event, her personal relationships with and memories of people involved in the case, personal interviews with offspring of those involved in the case who are no longer alive, as well as interviews with those who were alive at the time of many of the related incidents.

Newspaper accounts of events that occurred in 1955 and 2014 are also included in this memoir. Early reporting skirted unsavory truths that were later revealed by recollections of authorities and subsequently included in this memoir. Some reporting in the newspaper accounts differ from this narrative as this book is written from the empirical perspective, verbal accounts, and memories.

This is Ellen Suey's story. She lived it; it belongs to her. While in narrative form, it is true to the miraculous story as she and others remember it.

1

Richmond, Indiana and Wayne County

Wayne County in east-central Indiana was settled by families looking for a better life. Quakers came first in the early nineteenth century. They were seeking a peaceful existence free from slavery. They found it in a green, fertile place along a river they eventually named the Whitewater that ran through a deep, rocky, fossil-filled gorge. The land appeared flat; its rolling hills were smooth and gentle. There was plenty of game in woods filled with beeches, oaks, and walnut trees.

The Quakers agreed on a name for their town: Richmond. Their beliefs were built on orderliness, so they naturally plotted the city in square blocks. Streets running east and west were numbered; letters marked streets that ran north and south.

Soon factories appeared beside the Whitewater River. Many men became millionaires as inventors and entrepreneurs. Several turned the rich black dirt to highly productive farms.

Germans were the next to arrive, making their way north from Cincinnati. Most were skilled craftsmen who got jobs working for Quaker manufacturers. While the Friends were largely affluent and either lived on their own farmland or in mansions near downtown, their laborers built sturdy brick homes south of Richmond's Main Street.

The two groups were God-fearing, hard-working, and family-oriented. Both Christians, the Quakers worshipped in Meeting Houses while the Germans built Catholic and Lutheran Churches. They abided peacefully though separately, as they fiercely prized the same morals, ethics, and family bonds. They agreed on almost everything. Except temperance.

The National Road, later to become U.S. Route 40, connected eastern states with western and ran smack dab through the center of Richmond and Wayne County on to Indianapolis and beyond. U.S. Route 27 wound its way from the south northward. The intersection of these two important thoroughfares was Richmond. It only made sense to the Quakers to court a railroad and build a depot.

That's when the Irish arrived. Most built and then worked for the railroad. They developed their community in northeast Richmond, near the switching yard. Among the Irish were Methodists, Episcopalians, and devotees to the Pope. Churches were on nearly every corner. And two were Catholic, one for the Germans and one for the Irish.

Centerville, in the middle of Wayne County, had been the seat of government. But with all the county's industry and now the railroad located in the eastern-most city, Richmond leaders felt the honor belonged to it. Centerville put up a fight – there are still cannonball holes in one historic structure to prove it – but lost.

In 1881, E.G. Hill and his son Joseph created an entire industry built on the cultivation and breeding of roses, giving the city its nickname, the Rose City.

At the turn of the century, Richmond was largely still segregated, with Germans on the south side, Irish on the east side,

Quakers in the Starr District near downtown, and now Italians and blacks on the north side. But, by the twentieth century, newer Rose City residents and the working class began to create blended neighborhoods west of the Whitewater River.

In 1955, values instilled in the city by its founders still prevailed. Richmondites had a sense of Quaker attitudes and influences so subtle that it was rarely recognized. Most families worshipped at the church of their choice on Sundays. Fathers were steady wage-earners and held memberships in more than one service club such as Lions, Kiwanis and Optimists. Mothers were mainly homemakers. They maintained orderly households, watched Loretta Young Theater while their children napped and spent one or two evenings a month playing canasta or bridge with close friends.

By mid-twentieth century, there was a shift in family hierarchy. Children became the focus of postwar households. Products of the Great Depression and the war, parents were determined that their offspring would have carefree childhoods. They made sure of it.

Richmond had parks in every neighborhood. Children could choose from several sports leagues: Pop Warner football, YMCA basketball and Little League baseball. Tennis clubs were formed, a roller rink was built, two fathers opened a trampoline playground, and right on Main Street was Veach's, a toy store dedicated to children.

Central to the city of 35,000 was Glen Miller Park where kids could sled, make use of any number of swings, slides and teeter-totters, and throw pieces of bread to flotillas of ducks in a pristine lake. It had picnic gazebos, a band shell, a zoo with exotic animals, and even a miniature train so Baby Boomers could ride in circles around the playground.

In 1955 Richmond, it was all about the children.

2

September 22, 1955

Near U.S. 27, about fifteen miles south of Richmond is the rural community of Boston. Surrounded by rich farmland, the village lay at the crossroads of Route 122, which runs east/west, and the north/south Route 227 that became an Ohio highway just a few miles down the road.

Boston kids felt they were the lucky ones. Nearly all of them were being raised on large farms, in large families, with plenty of large barns and pastures to play in.

At the heart of the little town was Minnick's Restaurant. It opened before dawn for farmers to come in for coffee before their day began. This late September morning, there were more denim-clad world ambassadors than usual. It was raining, and raining hard. They wouldn't be able to get into their fields for at least another hour or two.

"Let's just hope it subsides by mid-morning," Oran Kitchel said. The land he farmed surrounding the small community airport would be ankle deep in mud. He lifted the spoon the waitress had set inside his ceramic mug to draw the heat from the coffee. He was tapping it on the lip of his mug when the door blew open, propelled by the stiff fall wind.

Julian Benner, Boston's town marshal, stumbled over the threshold as if he too were being blown into Minnick's. He shook rain from his slicker onto the restaurant's linoleum floor. "Whew. Not fit for man nor beast out there."

Not overly tall, and slender in build, Julian was just short of thirty. He kept his hair neatly trimmed though it was slightly thinning. He liked his neighbors and his job serving them, though that usually meant he might stop a speeder or two in a week's time. Brushing elbows with the farmers during early morning liars' sessions at Minnick's was more than part of the job.

"Sure hope you were all able to get your hay in before this downpour," he said, swinging one leg over the back of a chair and sitting down.

There were nods and groans.

"Well, one good thing about a day like this," Julian said, "is that bad guys tend to stay indoors. Won't be much happening today."

3

Corky Cordell kissed his wife Betty as if he hadn't been right down the hall most of the day. They'd lived in the residence attached to the ancient Wayne County jail near Richmond's downtown with their two young children since he'd been elected sheriff the year before.

"Let's make hay while the sun shines," he'd been told by an astute politician who knew well Corky's popularity throughout the county.

Corky was a Richmond police officer with the juvenile division when he'd been approached to run for sheriff. Children flocked to him. He loved them and they felt it. He liked nothing better than to seat a half dozen kids on the equipment box attached to the back of his police motorcycle to give them a ride. On his birthday one year, a group of Fairview neighborhood children gave him a birthday party and chipped in for a new white shirt.

It wasn't just kids who loved and trusted Corky. So did their parents. He'd been a natural leader from the time he was a boy. Maybe it was being sick for months, and nearly dying when a toddler, or the influence of a gentle grandmother, but Corky had a tender heart and ready smile. He was good-looking, with straight white teeth, curly dark hair, and cheerful blue eyes. Taller and more muscular than other boys his age, and a Golden Gloves champion, he'd never been a bully nor tolerated anyone who was.

So, when it was suggested he run for sheriff, though barely thirty years old, he did. A few months later he was conducting interviews in his living room, looking for a secretary. There were a lot of applicants to consider. But one evening he hired a frail young woman on the spot, without so much as checking a reference. Pauline Starr had come with her mother because heavy leg braces prevented her from driving. Before she even sat down on the Cordells' flowered sofa, she had the job.

This wet weekday it was quiet in the sheriff's office, with few calls and no emergencies. Still, Corky was ready for supper as he loosened his tan tie and relaxed the collar of his dark brown uniform shirt.

He was just peering into the black iron skillet, breathing in the peppery aroma of simmering pork chops, when the phone in the hall rang. He replaced the skillet lid, walked from the bright kitchen and picked up the heavy phone receiver. He was nearly always cheerful and it showed in his voice. "Gooood evening."

On the other end was the shaky voice of an elderly man. The young sheriff listened a moment then asked, "The baby's still alive? Did anybody stay with it – try to warm it, keep it safe?"

Corky was quiet, his face falling into grim concern. "I'm on my way," he said into the mouthpiece. "There's a deputy patrolling 27, though. He's closer. I'll send him right away.

"Meanwhile, get back to that baby!"

Sheriff Edward L. "Corky" Cordell

Luke 18:16 – *Jesus called the children to him and said, "Let the little children come to me, and do not hinder them, for the kingdom of God belongs to such as these."*

I always think of this verse when I think of how kids flocked to Corky.

Ellen Suey

4

The call to the Wayne County sheriff had come from the rural home of Paul Buckler. After finding a days-old infant, its lips and hands blue with cold, at the edge of a wooded and desolate field, a squirrel hunter and his teenage grandson had gone to the farmhouse for help. Buckler's was the first signs of life the hunter saw as he drove the county roads searching for a place that might have a phone.

It was once again the grace of God that the first residence that came into view was one with the lights on, indicating someone was home. After making the call to the county sheriff, the farmer, the hunter, and the teenager rushed back to the woods where the baby still lay in rain-soaked weeds covered only by a worn towel.

The baby blinked its eyes and helplessly moved its arms and legs in the air as if it were a turtle trapped on its back. Although blue, the infant was breathing but too weak to cry. The three men stood in a semicircle watching the baby become increasingly lifeless as they listened for a siren's wail.

As the infant weakly wriggled, its legs peeped from the towel. Its feet and toes were the same periwinkle blue as its lips and tiny hands. The towel, loosened by the soft squirming, fell away from the baby's left cheek and torso. The men gasped.

The child had been cut, and the ragged wound along the inside of its left forearm still seeped. But the appalling sight that caused the seasoned hunters and hardened farmer to swallow sickness was a plethora of writhing maggots voraciously feeding on the infant's jaw and ribs.

Large and round, the infant's eyes seemed to beseech the men. Its chin quivered. The faint sound of a siren wailed in the distance. The men standing over the baby turned their heads toward the sound.

Julian Benner, on his way home to supper, had heard on his police band radio the call between Corky and his deputy Dale Defibaugh. He turned his Ford Fairlane around and sped to the county road just a few miles away. He slammed to a stop in the middle of the road beside the hunter's car.

Julian sprinted the forty feet to the fence. "Where's that baby at?"

He was lifting his foot to climb the post when he stopped to turn toward the faint bawling of another siren. He chuckled, turning to the group on the other side. "Sounds like Corky's 'bout here. That didn't take long. Must've broke some speed limits."

The men's shocked silence at first confused Julian but then prompted him to follow their unbelieving eyes to the tiny mound in a blind of weeds at the foot of the fencepost. "Good Lord!"

Paul Buckler, taller than the hunter, leaned toward the fence and reached a hand to Julian to steady him as he climbed atop the post then jumped into the dripping weeds. The semicircle widened as the shivering hunters and farmer each took a step back.

John 14:18 – *I will not leave you as orphans; I will come to you.*

Each time I read or tell the story of how I was found, I am in awe of God's love. God guided the hunter and his grandson to where I was. God gave me the strength to cry out so they could hear me.

This shows me that God has immeasurable and abundant love for all His children. It tells me that I am someone and I am worth saving.

Having been found set my life on a whole different path than where it was heading. God gave me a do-over: someone else didn't think I was worthy, but He did.

I feel God gave me more compassion and caring for others from this experience.

Ellen Suey

5

A brown and tan Chevrolet Bel Air pulled to the side of the road behind the hunter's Chevy. It wasn't the Wayne County sheriff, but his deputy. A heavyset man with an intimidating personality heightened by his girth and stern expression, Dale Defibaugh heavily emerged from his vehicle then leaned back inside to retrieve his Stetson.

As he walked with purpose to the fence, he hoisted with bravado the waist of his uniform trousers, weighted down by a heavy braided-leather gun belt. He pushed the barbed wire down with his bare hands and stepped over.

Still in shock at the awful sight of parasites consuming the infant's tender flesh, the men standing above the baby silently stepped aside, pulling their jackets close against the damp chill. The hunter, his grandson, and the farmer were obviously in distress but the deputy ignored them as he bent his head to better see the infant.

Defibaugh's mouth dropped open.

Another siren grew increasingly loud then calmed as if it were a slowing Victrola recording as the sheriff arrived, braking to a stop behind his deputy's cruiser. Still with his tie loosened and shirt collar open, the sheriff stepped from the car, leaving his wide-brimmed hat on the seat. Walking briskly toward the fence, he studied the group, now openly distraught.

Instead of stepping over the barbed wire or climbing the post, Corky braced his right hand on the post as he leapt the fence and trotted to where the men mutely stood.

The soft pat of raindrops could clearly be heard falling from tall branches to lower ones, then finally to the bent shoulders of five silent men and sopping weeds around them. No one, including the soaked baby, was making a sound.

Corky bent down then raised up with the baby in his arms. He was visibly moved as he held what he knew was an obvious miracle. Time seemed to stand still. Seconds passed as the sheriff gently opened the towel to examine the infant. "A little girl."

He wrapped the sopping towel tightly about her. The sheriff nodded instructions to his deputy. Immediately Defibaugh pushed down the barbed wire and stepped over. With a delicacy that belied his boxer's physique, Corky gently handed the soaked bundle to Benner, who passed it to Defibaugh. The deputy hurried with it to his cruiser as if he were attempting a Notre Dame touchdown.

Defibaugh's patrol car sped away, its lights flashing and siren blaring. The rest of the men scaled the fence as if barbs didn't tear or scar. The farmer hurried to Julian's vehicle. Corky, lights and siren blaring, quickly caught up to his deputy. The town marshal with his passenger wasn't far behind. The hunter and his grandson took up the rear. It was a speeding caravan of cars, red lights twirling and sirens harshly harmonizing, rushing the ten miles toward Richmond and its hospital.

Julian Benner
(circa 1960; photo provided by his son, Dick Benner)

Deputies Horace "Mac" McCann and
Dale Defibaugh with Sheriff Corky Cordell

6

The parade of patrol cars, lights and sirens clearing the way, followed by the hunter's Chevrolet, raced from the outskirts of Boston through downtown Richmond. If it had been the next night, a Friday, the streets and sidewalks would be crowded. Main Street was the place to see and be seen on weekend evenings, whether folks were shopping or not.

Reid Memorial Hospital was named for the wife and son of Daniel Reid, a New York financier who'd grown up in Richmond. Though many Richmond residents and businessmen had raised money to construct the limestone hospital, Reid had come through with the balance needed to build the institution in 1905.

The hospital was located just on the northern outskirts of the city. Even when streets were crowded with traffic, it was barely five minutes from downtown. The Romanesque architecture of the massive hospital gave it a stately appearance. Inside, hallways were appropriately hushed. Nurses wore crisp white uniforms, starched caps and serious if not stern expressions.

It was just past seven in the evening when the four vehicles, the first carrying the tiny infant wrapped in a drenched towel, turned from U.S. 27 onto the hospital's circular drive. Standing outside the mammoth building awaiting her arrival were uniformed nurses and two emergency room doctors.

The group surged toward the cruiser's passenger side. A veteran doctor whose adrenaline at that moment overpowered his exhaustion yanked open the door and lifted the baby from the front seat. He hurried with her held tightly in his arms into the hospital.

Leaving his cruiser behind Defibaugh's, Corky asked the hunter to park his car then meet him in the waiting room. He and his deputy followed the doctors and nurses into a curtained emergency room cubicle.

They stood back, watching as the doctors painstakingly removed the baby from the towel, gingerly separating the umbilical cord from the terry cloth. The two were adhered by coagulated blood as if by stubborn glue. Only then did the doctors begin to examine her.

"Looks like bot fly maggots," the older doctor said, nodding to a nurse to take notes. "They're embedded in the flesh, not on it, so that means this little lady was probably out in the elements for at least two to three days. It's going to be quite a task to dislodge them. First, though, let's get her hydrated. Nurse, get some formula, please. This baby needs nutrients. She's in critical condition. It doesn't appear that she's had any attention whatsoever."

"It's a wonder," the younger doctor whispered, "she's survived. It does appear you're right; from the looks of the umbilical cord, she was placed in the towel immediately after birth and hasn't had any care at all. For days."

The nurse taking notes asked, "How do you know how old she is? She's so tiny."

The senior physician, furiously attending to the naked baby, spoke without looking up. He answered the question in a tigh growl. "These maggots don't just appear. They're laid by flies. They're larvae that have to hatch before they grow to this stage. And look at the damage they've already done. My estimation is she may be as much as five days old. It's a miracle she's alive."

"Do you think she was in the woods for that long?" asked the nurse scribbling notes.

"I have no idea," answered the examining physician. "She could have been in a house that had flies in it. Someplace in the country since those type flies are associated with livestock. If she was inside somewhere, somebody wrapped her in that towel right after birth and then didn't have anything to do with her again. For days."

He continued as if to himself, "I can't imagine."

"From the looks of this towel," said another nurse, "she was out in that hard rain last night. At the very least all day today. To have survived that was a miracle in itself. Forget how cold it was, wild animals in those woods, no nutrition of any kind . . ."

1 Peter 4:10 – *Each of you should use whatever gift you have received to serve others, as faithful stewards of God's grace in its various forms.*

I love when I hear "it's a miracle" the baby survived. I always look at it as God's plan and His love.

God showed me that all things are possible for those that love the Lord. My perspective is that my adoptive parents loved the Lord.

When I hear people say there is no God I say, "Let me tell you my story."

By the time I'm done there isn't a dry eye in the room and they now know there is a God.

Ellen Suey

7

Corky looked at the worn towel in the nurse's hands, dripping steadily onto the spotless linoleum. He asked that the towel be put in a plastic bag and brought to him in the waiting room. It was, as far as he knew, the only physical evidence that could lead to the criminal responsible for such a despicable act. Slipping out of the ante room, he walked with heavy tread and heart to talk with the two who'd found the forsaken infant.

Deputy Defibaugh, arms crossed, slumped against a nearby column. Corky asked the squirrel hunter, Clay Smith, how he'd found the tiny baby in the middle of nowhere. Smith told him that he had decided to hunt somewhere new that day, that he and his grandson had separated and had been in the woods from about ten that morning until six that evening. No, they didn't see or hear another living soul. Didn't see or hear a car all day long. Not even one passing by. And they'd both been quiet as church mice.

Smith recalled for Corky that they'd heard a strange sound just as they'd begun to field dress their squirrels. Curious, they'd decided to investigate.

As the hunter spoke, Corky recalled the distance from Smith's car to where the baby had been found. "It's a miracle that you could hear such a weakened baby from that distance. And you say she didn't make another sound, even as you walked along the fence row looking?

"The weeds were so dense and tall," Corky mused, "you'd have had to stop right over her or you would never have seen her."

He squinted his blue eyes in thought. "By the time I got there, the weeds were pretty tramped down. So you're saying they were high all around the baby when you found her?"

"Yes, sir. They were all real high with only her in the middle of 'em by the fence pole. Kinda by the base of that big tree. I'll never forget that tree."

The sheriff shook the hunter's hand and then held his hand out to the teenager, too. "It's a wonderment to me that God, Who created the universe, blesses ordinary people by using them in the most extraordinary ways. You two were the glove for God's almighty hand this day. I hope you always remember that."

8

After sending the hunters home, Corky and his deputy returned to the lonely road west of Boston. The two men used flashlights to find the empty nest near the base of the appropriately weeping tree, which stood as a wicked place marker. The weeds around that indentation were lying this way and that, the result of six pairs of feet trampling the area where the baby had lain.

"The hunter said all the weeds were tall around the baby," Corky told Dale. "And that baby had a nasty cut on the inside of her left forearm."

He tested one of the barbs of the wire fence. "I think somebody must have parked, walked over here and dropped her over the fence by the post. She must've been cut by the barbed wire as she fell. That would explain the wound on her arm."

"What explains those maggots?"

"Don't know. She might have laid here those days, or she might have been somewhere else where flies were attracted to the fresh blood. Her umbilical cord was matted to the towel. How could anybody keep a baby for days and not care for it? How could anybody leave it to die out here like this?"

He waved his flashlight toward the threatening woods, miles from city lights. "We can be pretty sure she was here all night for that towel to be so wet."

They didn't speak for several long seconds. Each knew the other's ghastly thoughts. Finally, the sheriff whispered as if the infant were still sleeping at his feet, "There's nothing we can see now. I'll bring Mac out here early tomorrow when there's light and we can see better."

The two returned to their cruisers. As Dale's crimson tail lights disappeared, Corky sat in his Bel Air with the ceiling light's soft yellow glow illuminating the sealed plastic bag holding the stained, soggy towel. He studied the beaded condensation sliding into a pool at its bottom.

Lifting the packet that held the sole link between the baby left to die and the one who left her there, he said as if in prayer, "The Lamb of God was surely holding you in His gentle hands, precious baby."

The spot where the helpless infant was dropped and left to die
(photo taken May 5, 2014)

9

September 23, 1955

Corky's chief deputy, Horace "Mac" McCann, was trapped by the sheriff's three-year-old daughter as he sat reading the morning paper in the upstairs bathroom of the Wayne County jail's attached sheriff's residence. He'd barely sat down and flipped open the Palladium Item when Mary Ellen had pushed open the door and padded in, her footed pajamas whispering across the lime-colored block linoleum.

She leaned against the bathtub, oblivious of the pool of dark fabric surrounding the deputy's feet. "MacAcan, what's the funnies say? Will you read 'em to me?"

Before he could answer, she said matter-of-factly, "I have a cowboy hat."

Stepping nearer to lean against his arm, she peered at the newspaper he held close to his lap. Bold headlines hovered above print so small she wondered how anyone could read it. Even if they knew how to read. "Whazit say?"

"Well, let's see . . ."

"Those big words. What's they say?"

"*Hunters Find New-Born Baby.*"

"A baby? Finded by hunters? Was they princes like in Sleeping Beauty?"

There was no answer. Mary Ellen looked from the newspaper to Mac's face. Under his clipped mustache, his lips were moving silently. She wondered at his expression. It was grim. Not like MacAcan at all. Tapping the small print, she demanded, "Read it to me!"

"It says the baby is a girl and is five to six days old. She was found by two hunters last night. She was taken to the hospital and, let's see . . . she's okay."

Thinking about the hunters, who were surely cut from Disney cloth, Mary Ellen asked, "Where was the baby finded?"

"They found the baby on a farm owned by Lyle Courtney," Mac read. He paused, shaking his head. "The poor little thing only had a towel around it, as cold and wet as it was yesterday."

"Oh, the poor little thing," Mary Ellen echoed softly, shaking her head.

"Wonder how long she'd been there," Mac said as if to himself. "Oh, here it is. Says your daddy said the baby had been lying there between twelve and twenty-four hours."

"Where's the pitchers at? What's that little baby girl look like, MacAcan?"

Seeing his chance for escape, Mac raised his eyebrows and smiled as if he had an idea for her. "Why don't you run wake up your daddy and ask him."

Three-year-old Mary Ellen Cordell dancing for
her father in front of the Wayne County jail's sheriff's residence
(captured from an 8mm home movie)

10
THE NEWSPAPER ACCOUNT

Palladium Item and Sun Telegram (front page)
September 23, 1955

Hunters Find New-Born Tot Lying In Woods

A baby girl five to six days old was found by Ind-122 north of Boston by two squirrel hunters Thursday evening and taken to Reid Memorial Hospital where it was reported in serious condition.

The hunters, Clay Smith, 331 South Henley Road and his 14-year old grandson David Hickman, found the baby in the edge of a woods on a farm owned by Lyle Courtney. Smith said the baby had only a towel around it.

Wayne County Sheriff Edward Cordell said the baby had been lying there between 12 to 24 hours. The towel the baby was lying on was wet indicating it had been there during Thursday morning's heavy rain.

Julian Benner, Boston town marshal, was called by Smith and rushed the baby to Richmond where he met Deputy Sheriff Dale Defibaugh who took the baby to the hospital. Smith said the baby's head was lying on the ground when they discovered it.

Smith said he and his grandson were dressing squirrels they had shot when they heard the baby cry. At first they thought it was a cat but later decided it was a baby and began to investigate.

The baby was found lying near the fence next to the road beside a large fence post. A gate into the woods was nearby but no tire marks were immediately found.

Cordell said there were no clues of where the baby came from or who abandoned it. Cordell also said there were no identification marks on the baby or the towel it was in. Union County Sheriff Rex Gilmore also investigated.

Cordell said he is continuing his investigation to find the mother of the child.

Sheriff Cordell said the baby weighed seven to nine pounds and apparently had not been born in a hospital.

He said all sheriffs have been alerted in the area, and the towel is to be checked for identification at a medical laboratory at Indianapolis.

Tiny Baby Girl Found In Woods At Boston

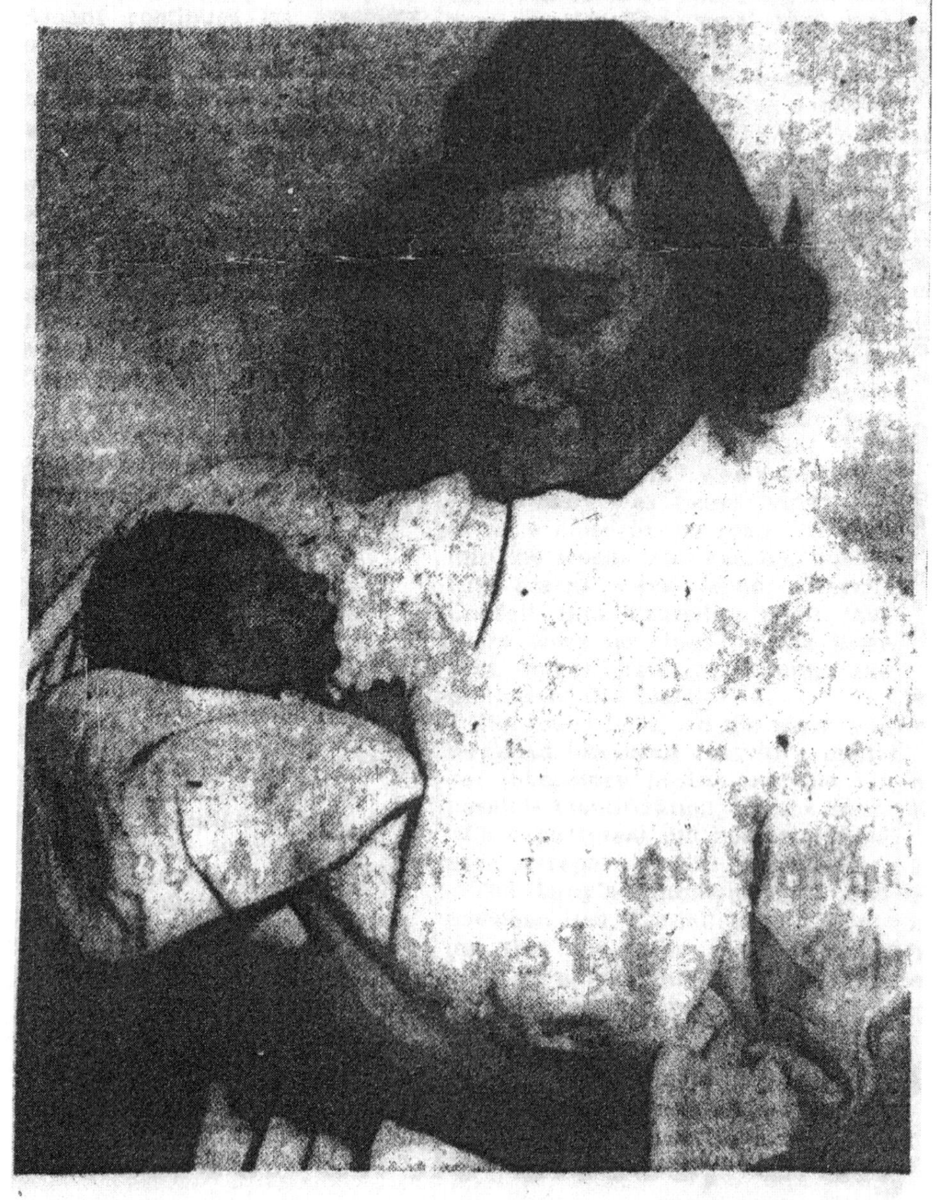

—Palladium-Item Photo

11

As downy clouds reflected pink and yellow over the dewy cornfield, two patrol cars pulled to the side of the deserted road. Mac wondered how the sheriff could have found this spot again. All these cornfields and woods looked alike. Corky was wondering how he'd ever forget it.

Both men approached the barbed wire fence. Corky pointed to the weathered post. "She was lying right on the other side. There's a gate over there a ways, but see, there aren't any tire tracks. None along this berm, either. Whoever left her, stopped on the road. Must have thought this looked like a lonesome place where they wouldn't be seen and she wouldn't be found. But they weren't wasting time by parking. Got a feeling they didn't even turn off the car."

Mac studied the prickly weed-covered ground on the woods' side of the fence, then turned his head to examine the mown grass between the fence and patrol cars. With this heavy dew, even a slight indentation would show up like velvet brushed the wrong way. His eyes moved to and fro over yards of weeds and grass, as far as he could see in all directions. All vegetation was undisturbed except for multiple footprints going to and from the road, and the few feet surrounding the post and under a nearby tree.

"Too many footprints. We'll never be able to distinguish the perp's from all the other ones. How many guys were here yesterday?"

"The hunter, his teenage grandson, a farmer, Julian, Dale and me. That's six."

"Well, I see lots coming to the post from the road. But nothing from the woods or cornfields. The weeds are only totally flat over there where everybody was standing by where the baby was. I wonder if the monster who did this returned to the scene of the crime. Maybe we could somehow get a footprint."

"No, not according to the hunter's description of the scene before all these weeds were trampled down yesterday. And there doesn't appear to be anything new. The only clue to whoever did this is that towel."

The sheriff tested the barbs on the top wire. "The hunter said the baby could hardly be seen in the thick weeds. That means she was, for all intents and purposes, hidden. We can imagine because we can easily see that no other weeds around her were disturbed."

"Left out here to die," Mac said with disgust.

"Worse," Corky said, tapping the razor-sharp barb, "I don't think whoever left her here laid her down gently. She's got a jagged, hairline cut about two inches long on the inside of her left forearm. More fresh than the birth trauma."

He continued reluctantly, "Whoever did this thing must have lifted her over the fence, but not quite high enough. One of these barbs cut her as she was dropped into the weeds."

"Couldn't lift her high enough," Mac mused. "Must've been the mother."

"Maybe not," Corky said, hoping that wasn't true. "Might have been a man in a hurry."

Mac peered over the fence to the oval indentation that still marked where the baby had fallen. "Miracle she landed face-up."

With a nod, Corky agreed. "One of many."

12

The sun was an orange orb over flat cornfields when the sheriff left his chief deputy to search for clues along the roadside, fence line, and into the deep woods. Transparent blue skies promised a drier day than the one before. Corky had told Mac he was headed back to the office to send the lone clue to the Indiana State Police laboratory in Indianapolis. But he had a stop to make first.

By the time he reached the hospital, the horizon was a buttery glow. He found head pediatrics nurse Jenny Parrish in her dimly-lit office near the nursery. She was surprisingly young for her responsible position. Pretty, with dark brown hair soft as a cloud that seemed to support her nurses' cap, Jenny's youth often comforted her young patients.

She was standing with her back to the doorway but turned at the faint sound of Corky's squeaking wingtips entering the still room. "Almost six and a half pounds," she announced as a greeting.

"Gaining weight already?" he asked.

"Not yet. At least I don't think so. This is her first official weighing. This little lady had quite a night. She's been fed, bathed and cuddled by just about everyone on the floor. She's still in very serious condition, though. It's going to take a while to remove the parasites. Most are embedded so thoroughly that it's going to be a very slow, delicate procedure. I'm afraid she'll have scars."

Corky winced. "Along her face?"

Nurse Parrish frowned, bleak confirmation that the damage was extensive, both along the baby's ribs and left jaw. She brightened, though, as she lifted the infant from the concave metal scales and handed her to the sheriff. "This is really what you came for, isn't it?"

Supporting the baby's head with one massive hand and cradling her back with the other, Corky put the foundling's little face to his cheek. So soft. He began to hum a lullaby, low and deep.

Jenny looked up from the baby's chart. "I think someone has somebody else wrapped around her finger."

Softly cooing into the baby's silky brown hair, "Ahhh-ah-ahhh," Corky nodded.

Jenny lifted her pen from the clipboard. "Any clue to her identity? We need a name for her chart."

Breathing in the tiny girl's fresh-bathed aroma, Corky said without hesitation, "How about Rose Wayne? Because she was found near Richmond, the Rose City. And because she was in Wayne County."

"Sounds like you've been thinking about this."

Swaying as he hummed, Corky merely smiled agreement.

"Rose Wayne it is," said Jenny, printing. "Birthdate? Any clue?"

"I'd like you to put down September 22, 1955, the day she was brought into our world. But from what the doctor said last night, her age could be anywhere from two to six days, judging by the condition of the, uh, parasites."

"Let's just say four days," Jenny said as she wrote in the date. "September 18, 1955."

Reluctantly handing Rose back to the head nurse, Corky said, "Wish I didn't have to go. But I need to get that towel over to the state police lab in Indianapolis."

Tester Photo

MISS JENNY SUE PARRISH

Here's a toast to the gal who made the fellows feel like Prince Charmings and Kings over all, when she was elected "Queen" of the Senior Hi-Y annual Queen of Hearts Ball.

Page 114

Jenny Parrish, Richmond Senior High School Queen of Hearts, 1948

13

Corky hadn't been gone long before the hushed pediatrics department began to fill with the curious as well as the official. Secure behind the plate glass of the nursery observation window, sleeping soundly among other infants in opaque basinets, Rose was peacefully unaware that she was the center of growing attention. Only medical personnel and Hazel Ball, supervisor of child welfare in the Department of Public Welfare, were permitted near her. Even the local newspaper and radio reporters were kept at a distance, garnering scant information from anyone who emerged from the cloistered pediatrics ward.

Reid administrators had, as soon as they realized the interest in, and notoriety of, their tiny patient, ordered that no distasteful or revealing details be divulged. Loose lips, someone joked darkly, would be to lose job. Only a handful of people knew the truth behind the infant's condition and the reason for her extended hospitalization, and none of them imparted that shocking fact to the media.

The next day, Saturday, September 24, the *Palladium Item* printed a picture of a smiling Jenny Parrish holding a tiny "unidentified" infant.

The story gave little new information from the article the day before, but informed readers that the baby was in fair condition and being ". . . *treated in much the same way as any other new-born would be treated. The little girl's temperature is down to normal and she has been eating well.*"

It recounted again that the infant had been found by hunters. New to the public was information that there were no visible clues, except the towel that had been wrapped around the baby had been sent for testing, ". . . *but the sheriff's department did not know how soon a report would be available.*"

In hopes that someone would come forward who could identify the mother, the sheriff had also given the press the information that the umbilical cord had not been tied, indicating the baby had not been born in a hospital.

1 Corinthians 2:9 – *That is what the Scriptures mean when they say, "No eye has seen, no ear has heard, and no mind has imagined what God has prepared for those who love him."*

It's overwhelming to read from the newspaper articles, and stories my mother told me, about all the love and attention I received at the hospital.

It's much the same as God's love for us. He loves us unconditionally.

It shows me how others loved me even if my biological mother couldn't. They loved me and they didn't even know me.

Ellen Suey

14
NEWSPAPER ACCOUNT

Palladium Item (front page)
September 23, 1955

Tiny Baby Girl Found In Woods At Boston

The Wayne County Sheriff's department continued its investigation Friday, trying to find the person or persons who left a five or six-day old baby girl at the edge of a woods north of Boston.

The baby, rushed Thursday evening to Reid Memorial Hospital, was reported in fair condition by hospital attendants. Its condition was much improved Friday over what it was when Deputy Sheriff Dale Defibaugh got it to the hospital at about 7:30 p.m. Thursday.

The tiny infant, whose weight was estimated by hospital officials at about six and one-half pounds, was found by two hunters near Ind-122 north of Boston. The hunters, Clay Smith, 331 South Henley Road, and his 14-year-old grandson, David Hickman said that the baby had only a towel around her when they found her.

Smith said that he and his grandson were dressing the squirrels they had shot when they heard the baby cry. At first they thought it was a cat but upon investigation found out otherwise.

Smith called Julian Benner, marshal of Boston, who rushed the baby to Richmond where he was met by Defibaugh.

Wrapped In Towel

Sheriff Edward Cordell said that the baby had been lying outside for from 12-24 hours before she was found. The towel that was wrapped around the baby was wet, indicating that it had been there during Thursday morning's heavy rain.

The hospital attendants said that they were treating the baby in much the same way as any other new-born would be treated. The little girl's temperature is down to normal and she has been eating well.

Deputy Sheriff Horace McCann spent all of Friday morning searching the spot where the baby was found for clues, but said that "nothing concrete" was uncovered.

The baby was found lying near a fence close to the road. A gate into the woods was nearby, but no tire marks were found. Sheriff Cordell said Thursday night that there were no clues on the baby that might help in finding the mother of the child.

The towel in which the baby was wrapped has been sent to a medical laboratory in Indianapolis for possible identification, but the Sheriff's department did not know how soon a report would be available.

The baby's umbilical cord had not been tied, Cordell said, indicating that the baby had not been born in a hospital.

15

September 24, 1955 – October 1, 1955

A headline in the *Cincinnati Enquirer* shouted with an exclamation point, "*It's Roseann Wayne!*" The subtitle, in slightly smaller point size, explained, "*Abandoned Baby Named For County Where She Was Found By Hunter In Woods.*"

Italics indicated the story was an *Enquirer Bureau Special* with the dateline "RICHMOND, Ind." The opening paragraph reported that ". . . (the baby found) *in a farm near Boston, has been named Roseann Wayne, the Wayne County Department of Public Welfare said today.*"

The story reported that the baby was in good condition and was being treated for ". . . *skin abrasions suffered apparently when she was lying on the ground.*"

It also said that the child had been placed under the custody of Judge Richard Kemper of Wayne Superior Court. For the first time, readers were informed that the only clue was a faint laundry mark on the towel that had been wrapped around the infant. There was, however, no word from the state police laboratory at Indianapolis where Sheriff Edward Cordell had sent the wet towel.

An article printed in the *Palladium Item* that day was nearly identical to the *Enquirer* story. It, however, reported a different malady: "*She is being treated for a skin rash.*"

The *Palladium Item* also included the misinformation that the baby would remain at the hospital until she gained weight. No news report mentioned that little Roseann Wayne had spent the past week, and would continue to stay a few more days, in Reid Memorial Hospital as doctors first removed dozens of maggots that had burrowed deep into and under her flesh, then tried everything in their power to help her heal without permanent disfigurement.

It would be ten full days before Roseann left Reid Memorial Hospital, bound for foster care in an undisclosed location. By that time, reporters had given up their constant queries. No one was talking to them. Secrecy draped like a curtain over any information that might shed light on the case of little Roseann Wayne.

16

Late October 1955

Mary Hart, a Department of Public Welfare caseworker, was given the task of finding a permanent home for the baby girl widely known for being found by hunters in the woods.

The first employee of the department nearly four decades earlier, Mary had a heart for children, and a way with them, too. In her mid-fifties, with dark wavy hair pulled loosely into a bun at the back of her head, she looked an unlikely child's advocate. But more than one child she'd placed for adoption had visited with her on the enclosed porch of her eastside home. She kept a Desert Rose patterned cookie jar filled and waiting for just those visits.

One youngster who knocked on her door had run away from his adoptive home. She told him he looked thirsty, offered him lemonade and wisely waited as he munched on one of her freshly baked oatmeal cookies for him to tell his story. She smoothed and soothed. He finally decided to return home.

"You'd think finding a family for Roseann would be easy," Mary told Corky Cordell a month after the infant was found. "We've had hundreds of requests. Yours included."

The sheriff had been a regular visitor to Mary's office, confident that like most everyone else, she could be won over. It had always been easy for Corky to make and keep friends, with his easy-going disposition. Like Will Rogers, he never met a man he didn't like. And because everyone felt it, they liked him back.

But Mary was firm. "I just can't do it, Corky. It's a rule I can't break, especially with this little girl. She's had too much publicity. Why, she'd be dogged all her life by that awful story; she wouldn't have a chance at a normal life. We can't let Roseann stay in Indiana. The challenge is going to be finding someone who wants a baby, can keep a secret and hasn't bombarded us with inquiries about this specific child."

Corky grinned sheepishly. Mary laughed and patted his shoulder affectionately. "I don't mean you. We all know you love Roseann. But you can't have her unless you're willing to move, oh, maybe about a thousand miles from here. Don't worry, though, we won't let just anybody adopt her. I'll not rest until I find that right couple who I know will love her just because she's theirs."

Defeated, the sheriff walked the two blocks from Mary's office to his own. His secretary, Pauline Starr, looked up from her desk as he came in the door. Heavy metal arm-braces were propped against the wall behind her. The victim of childhood polio, Pauline was able only to swing her legs one at a time in a slow, stilted fashion that marginally resembled walking. She was rarely seen without her braces gripped by determined fists, or her signature toothy grin.

Deputies carried her up the carved stone steps into the Italianate building each morning, then back down again each evening. Inside the office, a swivel chair on rollers enabled her to conduct business in any part of the offices or jail corridors. Prisoners and trusties alike popped eager faces from cells and duties when they heard the rhythmic sound of wheels against slate or the hollow tap of her rubber-tipped braces.

Pauline lifted a large manila envelope from her desk. "You've been waiting for this. It came in the morning mail."

Corky read the return address: "Indiana State Police."

The sealed flap had been carefully cut by a letter opener. "What's it say, Pauline?"

"Now, Cork, you know better than that. I didn't read it."

He slipped a single flat document from the envelope and quickly skimmed the brief report. "Well, there's something we can follow up on, but not much. That washed out laundry mark was identified as being from the Gibson Hotel in Cincinnati."

Pauline whistled. "Fancy. Must've been somebody with influence. Maybe from Ohio. Do you think that baby was born there?"

She sounded doubtful.

So was the sheriff. "We can check their guest registry for dates just prior to September twenty-second. Because the towel was so faded, my guess is the towel was stolen. Maybe years ago.

"It says here that there were two hairs on the towel. A person's, uh . . ." he hesitated.

His spinster secretary raised her eyebrows. She liked to tease him, but this she knew was too embarrassing for him to say aloud: that the hair was pubic. So she asked innocently, "And what was the other?"

Quizzically, Corky answered, "A dog's."

Pauline Starr
(Circa 1966 in Mayor E.L. Cordell's office, her arm braces against the wall behind her)

John 14:18 – *I will not leave you as orphans; I will come to you.*

It was amazing the number of people who wanted to adopt me. A child that wasn't planned nor wanted was now wanted by many.

God knew all along that He had the perfect family waiting and wanting me. I couldn't imagine living in any other family except for the one God had chosen. I never gave it a second thought about how people may have treated or acted towards me if I had been adopted to a family in Richmond. God knew.

There was a dog hair discovered on the towel that was around me in the woods.

I have always loved dogs and have had up to four at one time. Is that because of the dog involved in my time in the woods? Did God send a dog to stay with me and protect me? To keep me warm? That won't be answered till I see the Lord again.

I was walking one day and came across a dog that was spinning in circles and bumping the curb. I told my husband I needed to check it out. Turned out the sweet little guy was blind. Someone had dumped him. Sound familiar?

I just had to take him home and get him groomed and give him a loving home. That sweet little guy reminded me of myself many years ago and how others helped me.

God has a plan for each of us. Sometimes we need to sit, listen and wait. His plans far exceed whatever plans we may come up with.

Ellen Suey

17

November 1955

It was too late in the evening to be alone in the cavernous, dark court house. Mary Hart replaced a stack of files in the metal cabinet, careful to keep them in alphabetical order. With a sigh she closed the drawer and locked it. She looked at the plain round clock on the wall above the door. Almost midnight.

"Time to go home," she said to herself, turning from the file cabinet. Taking her soft cloth coat from the hall tree beside the door, she hesitated. "Maybe I should stay and get it over with. I only have two more files."

Raising her eyes again to the clock, she shrugged on the coat. "I'll start fresh tomorrow with 'T' and then finish by noon. Surely there has to be someone in those past adoption records who fits Roseann's need."

Thanksgiving was nearing. The baby was doing remarkably well and it was time to place her in a permanent home. By the grace of God, Mary thought, Roseann was not only alive but also healthy earlier than expected from the looks of her dire condition those first weeks.

The next morning Mary unlocked the file cabinet and carried the 'T – V' folder to her desk. She was just opening the mottled green folder when the phone rang.

"Mary, this is Merwin Test."

She at once smiled. Ah, yes. Stoic, reserved Merwin and friendly, out-going Marga, the quintessential opposites-attract who formed a seamless union. Raised a Quaker, Merwin was dependably reticent but kind when speaking of others. Marga, with her pretty green eyes, was the oldest of three home-schooled children and unreservedly enjoyed people around her. They were devoted to one another, and to the baby boy they'd adopted from the Wayne County Welfare Department two years earlier.

Mary opened the folder on her calendar desk pad and reached to turn on the desk lamp. The florescent light shone like a beacon on the promising Test file.

"Why hadn't I thought of them before?" she thought in the brief moment of silence as Merwin waited to hear her return his greeting. The Tests live in Silver Spring, Maryland, she thought, far from Richmond. Merwin is a physicist at the Naval Ordinance Lab. He works for the Department of Defense, so we know he can keep secrets. And so can Marga. She worked for the government in institutional management in D.C. Can't get more hush-hush than the capitol.

Mary smiled into her telephone mouth-piece. "It's so nice to hear from you. How is Marga? She faithfully sends us reports. Never misses a date or deadline. I so enjoy the pictures she sends us of little John. And Christmas cards, too."

"Well, that's why I called. Marga and I would like to adopt a little girl."

Mary's heart leapt. "I'm glad you called. We have an unusual case here that needs special treatment. About three months ago, a baby girl was found by hunters in the woods near Boston. She was left to die and was close to it when she was found. Her injuries were such that she was hospitalized for ten days. She's been in foster care since.

"She's received a lot of notoriety on radio, newspaper and television due to the circumstances surrounding her abandonment. So, it's a requirement that she must be adopted outside the state of Indiana."

Mary barely paused to take a breath. "To the best of our ability, we've established that she was born September 18 and by the time she was found weighed only six . . ."

"We don't need to hear any more," Merwin said. "Marga and I want to adopt her."

Mary Hart
(Photo provided by her daughter, Janet Hart Heinicke)

Isaiah 49:15 – *Can a mother forget the baby at her breast and have no compassion on the child she has borne? Though she may forget, I will not forget you!*

The part where my dad says he doesn't want to hear anymore always makes me cry. It's a good cry because it shows he loved me before he even saw me.

God loved us before He ever saw us.

My folks always loved me unconditionally. My mother had a saying posted on her refrigerator till the day she passed away:

You could not be flesh of my flesh,
Bone of my bones,
Yet you've become a part of me—
Child of my own.
You could not fill the empty womb,
Nor was I blessed
To feel the first faint stir of life
Beneath my breast.
Yet you drew forth the warmth and love
God has instilled,
Within a Mother's yearning heart
When arms were filled.
Regardless of the way you came,
I must confess.....
I could not love you any more,
Nor any less.

Author unknown to me, Ellen Suey

18

December 27, 1955

Skies were clear and it was below freezing that Tuesday. A light snow had fallen the night before, but not enough to prevent traveling 20 miles from Richmond on Route 40 to Cambridge City, Indiana. Merwin and Marga Test were anxiously waiting at the western Wayne County home of Merwin's parents for the arrival of their new daughter.

Hazel Ball stayed in the car to keep the heater running as Mary Hart went inside the foster family's Richmond home to gather Roseann and her belongings. The foster family who had cared for and grown to love her had ignored the frigid temperatures to dress her in the lightweight blue dotted Swiss dress that the sheriff's entire staff had chipped in to purchase.

They'd been told Corky had picked it out because ". . . it matched Rose Wayne's eyes."

Back in the car, holding Roseann tight in her arms, Mary said to her supervisor, "We have to make a stop first. I need to see somebody."

Hazel couldn't help herself; she laughed. "Who do we know who always says that?"

Mary laughed, too, thinking of the sheriff and the words he inevitably uttered any time anyone was with him in his cruiser.

Hazel pointed the car in the direction of the old county jail on South Second Street.

Corky was at his desk in his small office behind Pauline's. A neighbor, Joyce Melling, was talking to Pauline when the two welfare workers entered, carrying Roseann. Pauline pushed the swivel chair away from the desk and leaned to her left to peek around her visitor to greet the newcomers.

"Why, what have you got there?"

"We brought her to say goodbye," Hazel answered, stepping toward the desk. "She's going to meet her new parents today."

Looking into the blanket as Hazel passed Roseann to Pauline, Joyce said, "What a beautiful baby! I don't think I've ever seen such a pretty little mouth. It's like a little rosebud."

Unused to infants, Pauline held Roseann stiffly but her grin gave away her delight. "Look, she's wearing our Polly Flinders dress! What a little doll. She couldn't be any sweeter."

By then the sheriff had emerged from his office. Hazel and Mary could see that his smile was forced, not the usual open grin that showed both rows of smooth, straight teeth. He held his arms out toward Pauline, who relinquished the baby. Pressing Roseann close to his cheek as he'd done three months before in Jenny Parrish's office, Corky swayed for more than a few moments in a lullaby waltz. It was as if he were unaware or didn't care that four women were looking on.

He kissed Rose Wayne's forehead and handed her to Hazel. He never referred to her as Roseann. To him, she would always be Rose Wayne.

As much as the Wayne County Department of Welfare had thrilled the sheriff that morning, they were disappointing Roseann's new family.

"I'm sorry," Hazel told Merwin and Marga again. "It's so very important that no one connect your baby with the one found in the woods. I do apologize that I didn't make it more clear. You must leave with her no later than tomorrow. Take her back to Maryland, and don't let anyone else see her before you leave. As an excuse, say she has a cold."

Merwin, watching Marga as she cuddled their new daughter on the sofa in the front room of his parents' Cambridge City home, sighed. He knew his wife and step-mother had planned a small get-together the next day to introduce their daughter to Indiana friends and family.

"No one else can see her?" he pleaded.

"I'm afraid not. There's been so much publicity."

Marga let a disappointed sigh escape her downturned lips. "Just a few family, then?"

Hazel shook her head.

The very next day, without being allowed to show anyone their darling new baby, Merwin and Marga began the long drive back to Silver Spring, Maryland. John played in the back seat and little Mary Ellen Test was held tight and close to her mother's bosom.

The Tests were already proving that despite their own wishes, they would strictly adhere to those of the Wayne County authorities. And they would also prove many times that they could indeed keep secrets.

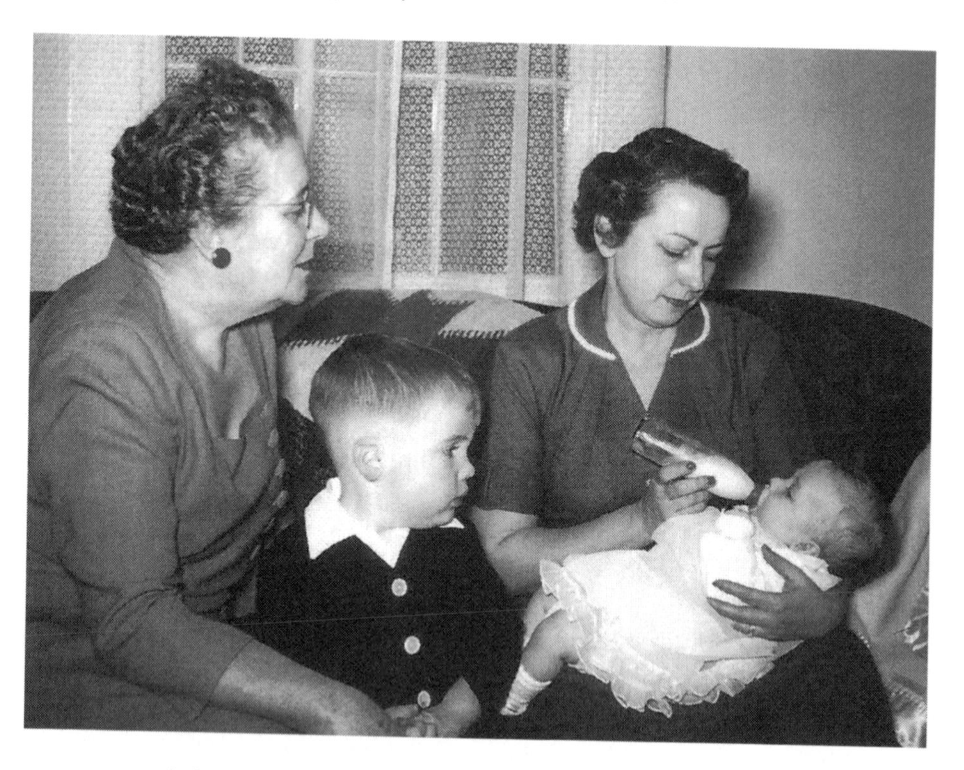

Marga Test with Ellen, December 27, 1955,
as her mother-in-law and son look on

19

December 21, 1956

The ghosts always followed the same path. They came into her room through one of the tall double-hung windows that faced the street, flew toward the door to the jail residence's upstairs hallway, then turned past it around the room, glowing white across the wall above her trundle bed. Just as swiftly as they came, they disappeared.

Mary Ellen Cordell had watched a lot of them fly into and out of her room since the train passing behind the jail and its attached residence had awakened her with its warning wail as the C&O approached Main Street. She was only in nursery school so couldn't count that high, but there had been lots and lots. Sometimes they came in pairs. Other times she'd think the parade was over, then just as she was nodding off another bright ghost hurried through.

Here came another one, this one a bit slower than the rest. What was going on, she wondered, a ghost dance and her bedroom was a ballroom? She wasn't scared, just curious. "Daaaddy," she called. "Daddy, come here."

She couldn't know it was a hair past midnight. Even if she had known her parents were sound asleep across the hall, though, she wouldn't have hesitated to call out to Daddy. He always came.

"What's the matter?" Corky asked, rubbing both eyes at once with the palms of his hands.

"There's ghosts."

"Ghosts? Where?"

"In my room. They keep coming in and flying around and then leaving."

He sat on the edge of her undersized bed. "I don't see any ghosts here."

"Yes-huh. They come in that window over there."

He humored her, sitting quietly, watching the far window. Nothing. Not one. "See, there aren't any ghosts," he said, pulling her blanket around her shoulders.

Disappointed, Mary Ellen protested. "There were lots of 'em a minute ago. See! Look, there's another one!"

The glowing specter was already moving past the doorway. Her father laughed. "That's not a ghost. It's a car's headlights from the street. That's what you've been seeing; car headlights."

"No, they're ghosts. Cars can't drive on walls."

"Wait. When the next one comes, listen. You'll hear a car go by outside. Its headlights will move across the room as they pass by."

She did and they did. Daddy was right. The next ghost that flew around her room was accompanied by the sound of a car's tires on the street outside. Corky leaned down, gave her a kiss, and chuckling, stood.

"Read me a story."

"No, it's too dark," he said, smoothing her cheek with his index finger then tickling her ear. But instead of leaving, he sat beside her again, his knees to his chest. "How about I tell you one?"

He had a deep voice that vibrated and soothed. "This is a true story. It's about a little girl named . . . "

"Mary Ellen?" she asked hopefully.

"No. Not in this story."

"Oh."

"But she's a very pret-tee little girl. Just like you."

His daughter giggled, and he went on. "When she was just a tiny little baby somebody left her under a tree where they thought no one could find her. It was cold, very cold. And it rained all night long.

"The next day the little baby lay under the tree all day long. Even though it stopped raining she was very wet. And very cold."

Mary Ellen was fascinated. This was just like a Disney story. "Did the tree protect her? Did the forest animals come make her safe and warm?"

"I don't know. Maybe a friendly dog came and kept her safe and warm during the night."

"What happened to the pretty little baby when the sun came out?" She imagined her lying at the foot of a friendly tree in a basinet with frills just like the one in *Lady and the Tramp*. A scruffy dog sat alert and straight next to it, on guard against the wicked people who had left her there.

"But late that day, just as the sun was setting, a hunter found the baby."

"A hunter? This sounds like a story MacAcan told me. Was he a prince like in *Sleeping Beauty*?" She could see the hunter again, handsome and wearing a Peter Pan hat with a feather. A bow and a quiver of arrows were slung over his shoulder. She liked this story.

"He was an ordinary man. Just a hunter. But he knew the baby shouldn't be there, so guess who he called?"

She shook her head. When you're the hero, why would you need to call anybody?

"Me."

"You?" Of course. That made sense.

"And did you go get the little baby, Daddy?"

"Yes. But she was very cold and very sick. So I took her to the hospital where they made her all better."

Mary Ellen smiled, gratified. A happy ending.

But her father went on. "I got to name her. Rose for Richmond . . ."

"Rose isn't Richmond."

"But Richmond is the City of Roses."

"Oh."

"And Wayne for Wayne County. I named that little baby who was found by the hunter under the tree Rose Wayne."

"Where is she now?"

"I don't know. But we can always ask Jesus to protect her, wherever she is."

"Okay," she said, folding her hands. "I'm ready."

Mary Ellen Cordell in Pauline Starr's swivel chair
in the sheriff's office (circa 1956)

20

Marga Test struggled to pull the eyelet lace bonnet over Ellen's soft brown curls. Her sister, Ruth Shendler, balanced the wriggling baby on her lap. They were sitting in the living room of the Shendler's bungalow near Boston, Indiana. The sisters, just fourteen months apart, had been home-schooled as children and were the best of friends, though they lived hundreds of miles apart.

Watching her three small cousins chase each other around the free-standing Christmas tree in the Shendler's living room, Ellen wanted down. At fifteen months old, she was able to happily toddle after the older children. Being held captive while Mommy and Aunt Ruth fussed over her was no fun at all. "Hold still, sweetheart," Aunt Ruth said, her grasp more firm than her tone.

Ellen reached a chubby hand to the bonnet crown, clenched it in all five dimpled fingers and lifted it off, dropping it to the floor. She laughed. This was almost as entertaining as stumbling after the kids playing tag on the other side of the doorway.

Marga retrieved the bonnet from the floor with a sigh. This game was not fun for her at all. Ruth attempted to distract her niece by combing her fingers gently through Ellen's silky curls. "What are these bare places on Ellen's head?"

"We noticed them when her hair began to thicken," Marga said dismissively, tugging the hat on before Ellen could grab it again. She pretended she didn't know they were a reminder of the same parasites that'd left their mark on the baby's soft neck. It was hard for her to keep such a secret from her closest friend and sister, so she said flippantly, "I have no idea what caused them."

Marga knotted the bonnet's satin ribbons then tied a thick bow slightly to the left of Ellen's chin. She fluffed out the bow. It was an effective method of hiding the shiny rose scar that ran thickly along Ellen's jawline, from chin to ear. It was a ploy that was never questioned since most babies' bonnets were similarly tied.

"And this scar," Marga worried, pushing her hands against her knees to stand. "It's worse now. I don't know what Mrs. Hart will say. Maybe she won't notice."

"Mrs. Hart? What has she to do with it?"

"We had to get her permission for the surgery last February. The doctor thought that the scarring could be reduced if he operated on it while the wound was still healing. We'd only had her a little over a month. She was still a ward of the court, so we had to have Mary's permission. But I'm afraid he made it worse."

"No one will be looking at her scar, Marga. She is too pretty for that!" Ruth gave Ellen a kiss on her pillowy cheek before handing the child to her mother. "Did Mrs. Hart ever tell you how Ellen was hurt?"

Marga bussed her daughter's other cheek then nuzzled her nose in an Eskimo kiss. She shrugged. How she would love to confide in her sister. "I suppose there are a lot of children who come to Mrs. Hart with wounds of one kind or another. I'm just thankful that this is the kind that will heal. That she doesn't appear to have any injury beyond these reminders on the outside. And that God chose us to be her parents."

"Well, today it's official!" Ruth looked at the Longines watch on her wrist. "You'd better get going. The hearing's in a half hour."

Ruth was right; Mary Hart didn't notice the yawning pink scar that ran just under Ellen's baby-soft jawline. If she even remembered writing the letter nearly a year ago giving permission to try to repair the maggots' damage, she didn't let on. This occasion was too happy. She'd hardly ever seen the customarily reserved Merwin smile, let alone grin. Marga, tracks of earlier tears streaking her powdered cheeks, was beaming.

Ellen wriggled against Mary's affectionate hold. The baby reached out her arms and leaned away from Mary Hart's embrace. She wanted her mother. It was as if she knew that just an hour ago she'd formally become Mary Ellen Test in a brief but extraordinarily joyful hearing in the closed chambers of Judge J. Richard Kemper.

"Here it is," Marga said, proudly showing the Wayne County Welfare Department case worker the document decorated with the embossed state seal of Indiana.

Palms up, she wriggled her fingers, playfully beckoning her laughing daughter, then accepted her from Mary. "Thank you for choosing us, Mrs. Hart. We had to come right over to thank you in person just as soon as the gavel hit the desk."

Several minutes after the Test family left her office, Mary was still smiling as she placed a writ in their file. "Strange," she said to the empty room, "this seems so impersonal and cold: Case Number 104, Superior Court One. There was certainly nothing cold about the seventh heaven that just walked out that door."

Locking the cabinet, she mused that the adoption paper looked like the hundreds of others she'd seen. Merwin and Marga appeared as elated as the hundreds of other new parents who'd come through her office. Yet, thinking how the cherubic baby so naturally cuddled in her mother's arms, with her father firmly enfolding both of them in his, Mary was keenly aware that this adoption was the most miraculous she had seen or would likely ever see.

She couldn't help but think as she returned to her desk, though, that a little over a year ago this case was also the most appalling she had ever experienced.

She hoped to never witness another like it.

21
1957

Mary Ellen Cordell heard her daddy coming up the long winding staircase at the end of the hall. She wanted to get out of bed and run to him as he stepped into the upstairs hallway. She liked how he grabbed her up to give her tickle-kisses under her chin, and how wonderfully comforting his Old Spice aftershave lotion smelled. She breathed deep just thinking about it.

But she'd already been warned by her mother to not get out of bed again. The last time was with a swat to the heiny-booble. She listened for Daddy to come in to check on her. But instead she heard him go into his own room, dropping his gun belt to the floor just inside the door.

"It was worse than I'd suspected," she heard him whisper to her mother.

"What could be worse than three starving, neglected children?"

They were talking quietly, but Mary Ellen could hear them plain as day. She heard the mattress springs squeak as her Daddy sat down. One shoe dropped heavily to the hardwood floor. Then the other.

"There were two babies in one crib. I won't describe it to you. You wouldn't sleep. One little girl was about two years old. The other an infant. Just a tiny thing."

Both Mary Ellen and her mother waited. Was Daddy crying? "I carried the baby out of there, with her sister in the baby bed calling 'Tina' over and over, until I was clear out the front door and almost in the cruiser. Nearly broke my heart. Rushed the baby to Reid, but she was dead on arrival. Something I was pretty sure about already.

"I'll go back tomorrow to remove the other two little girls. There was another one, about three years old. I'd have gone back to get them already, but legally I can't. We'll have to get a court order and get county welfare involved. Mary Hart will have to go along.

"How can anyone do anything like that to children? To a helpless baby?" he asked without expecting his wife to answer. There could be no answer; they both knew that.

Mary Ellen heard him mention another name. The little girl who'd kept calling for her sister.

Her parents were quiet, then she heard her father walking softly toward her room in his stocking feet. "Daddy?" she said as his form created a shadow from the hall light that fell across her bed.

"What are you doing still awake?"

"I was waiting for you, Daddy."

Corky sat on the edge of her bed, bent over and kissed her forehead. He sighed in a way that was new to her.

"Daddy, are you sad? I heard you ask Mommy how anybody could do anything like that to a little baby. Somebody hurt a baby? And she died? That happens?"

"Sometimes."

"Who did it?"

"Well, sometimes parents will hurt their own baby."

Mary Ellen was too astounded to ask anything more. After saying a prayer together as they did every night, her father kissed her again. He left the room, careful to leave her door open just enough that a sliver of yellow light crossed the floor and shone onto her bedcovers. Her hands still pressed together as if in prayer, she quietly crooned a new favorite song.

"I hear the cottonwoods whisperin' above, Tammy ... Tammy ..."

22

"Rock-a-bye baby, in the treetop; when the wind blows, the cradle will rock; when the bough breaks, the cradle will fall; And down will come Ellen, cradle and all."

Marga Test sang the nursery rhyme to her baby nearly every evening just before tucking her into her crib. Sometimes she cradled her in the bentwood rocker. Other nights she would sway and sing just before lying Ellen down. But always she tagged on a whispered closing she'd created so her daughter would always know, and never have to be told, that she was chosen especially for them.

"And guess who caught her?" she asked her sleepy daughter, happy expectation in her voice. "Mommy and Daddy! She landed right in our arms for us to love and adopt."

Marga nuzzled and kissed her daughter's nose and cheek. "Ellen's our little girl."

23

1960

Ellen Test pretended to skip an invisible hopscotch on the sidewalk. When she got to a crack, she was careful to jump over.

"Break your mother's back" she sing-songed before hopping and dancing onto the next square of cement. It was her third day of kindergarten and her mother had allowed her to walk home with the neighbor children and her brother John, who was two years older. She trailed behind them, oblivious to their chatter as she concentrated on the imaginary magic squares and the cracks between them.

The tree branches in Maryland were still full, though some had begun to show tints of yellow or orange. The Moses bushes were already turning crimson. Ellen liked the way the shadows from the canopy of branches that hung over the sidewalk played on the plaid of her skirt. Her mind was on hopscotch, red bushes and dappled shadows when she nearly collided with a third grader blocking her game.

The older children had stopped, hands on hips. "Hurry up, slow poke. We're not babysitters, you know."

"Yeah. Especially for somebody nobody wants," sneered another.

Ellen's mouth formed an O. This was news to her. She looked for her brother, but he was no longer with the group of neighborhood children. She was on her own. "Yes I am. My mommy and daddy want me."

"They're not your real mommy and daddy," a boy hoped to inform her.

"I know," she said, not giving him satisfaction.

"You don't know your real parents. Wanna know why? 'Cause they didn't want you. They dumped you on the ground. They just dumped you and left you."

Ellen's face crumpled into a tearful mask, her eyebrows scrunched inward and her bottom lip trembled. She wanted to say something back, but couldn't think of anything. Instead, she bolted into the grass beside the sidewalk, circumventing the taunting children. She ran the half block to her house where she knew her mother would be waiting for her, an after-school snack already set for her and John on the Formica table.

She was nearly hysterical by the time she pushed the back door open to run screaming into the kitchen. "Mommy! Mommy! They said nobody wanted me."

Marga turned from the sink where she'd been snapping fresh green beans for supper. She knelt on the linoleum to take her daughter into her outstretched arms. Ellen blubbered into her shoulder. "They said I was dumped and left!"

Marga froze, and Ellen felt it. Quieting, she leaned back and blinked away tears to peer questioningly into her mother's eyes. Marga looked as if she'd been struck between the shoulder blades. Her face had paled, her eyes were painful islands in a sea of white and her mouth was slack. It seemed forever to the little girl before her mother took a breath. Ellen shifted to sit in her lap, her arms still around Marga's neck.

"Who said you were . . . what did they say?" her mother asked, purposefully calm.

"Those kids. Mark and Tonya and them," Ellen said through hiccupping sniffles. "They said that nobody wanted me. That my real parents dumped me and left me."

Holding Ellen tight, Marga kissed the top of her head and moved Ellen's legs across her own knees so she could see her daughter's face. She kissed her damp cheeks and brushed away tears that clung to Ellen's dark lashes.

"You know that's not true. Daddy and I want you. We wanted you so much that we went all the way to Indiana and brought you home with us."

"But what about those other people who dumped me and left?"

Marga was very still. She could hardly breathe. No one in this neighborhood, in this town, in this state, could possibly know that. Only Merwin's parents knew why they'd been allowed to adopt Ellen. The only other person they'd told was Marga's brother Gordon. They felt he should be aware of her ordeal because he was to be the children's guardian should anything happen to them.

She hadn't even told Ruth! No, she was certain that these naughty children had merely somehow guessed the truth.

"Ellen, you mustn't listen to these mean things. They're not true. First, you know good and well that Daddy and I are your real parents, and that we want and love you. And second, who in the world would dump such a sweet little baby and leave her?"

Ellen looked into her mother's face. It was transformed back into the one she recognized. Not horrified like before, but pleasant and relaxed. She ran a freckled forearm across her nose then upward over her cheek. She quieted the last of her sniffles, then laid her head against her mother's shoulder, suddenly sleepy. She sighed. Marga tilted Ellen's chin to look into her blue eyes.

"Can I see a smile?"

Ellen at home in Maryland, in charge of the store

24

Never mind the pale white patch spreading a web under her left jaw. Or the Maginot Line of scars running along her ribs and the jagged ridge on her forearm that'd been there ever since she could remember. Eight-year-old Ellen Test was becoming a patchwork of scrapes, scabs and scars. It seemed that every time she turned around she was getting sewn up after one calamity or another.

Ellen nearly lost a finger when she grabbed a butcher knife her brother had playfully stuck into the backdoor screen. During a family picnic in Williamsburg, Indiana, she was chasing her brother when she fell and subsequently received stitches in her knee.

Another time, the two siblings were playing with her metal doll house. Ellen doesn't remember what started the argument, but it ended with a visit to the emergency room to stitch up a gash left by the toy's sharp aluminum roof.

"Mommy," she said, delicately fingering ten stitches above her right eye, "sometimes I feel like I'm held together by thread."

In addition to scars and stitches, it seemed Ellen was nearly always tattooed with bruises and scrapes. During one scheduled check-up, the doctor, aware of Ellen's infant abuse, angrily confronted Marga about the number of colorful injuries. "How did this child get these marks?"

Mortified, Marga was speechless. Ellen piped up, informing the physician that she was learning to ride a bike. For years, Marga said with a chuckle, "I was never so happy that she opened her mouth!"

More than a few times, Ellen asked her mother how she'd gotten her early scars, the ones she didn't remember getting. Marga always waved the question away. "Sometimes when you adopt children, they have scars when they come to you."

Today, she knew exactly why she was visiting the podiatrist. Nothing serious that called for another trip to the emergency room, but her mother knew it couldn't wait.

"All the other girls are going swimming today," Ellen complained.

"You've had enough sun anyway, dear. You have more freckles than Alfalfa."

Ellen laughed, thinking about the comical Little Rascal.

She laughed again when the doctor came in to examine her. He sat on a three-legged rolling stool and took Ellen's bare foot into his lap. Before looking at her abrasion, though, he appeared to be shocked by something on her face. "What happened to you?" he asked in exaggerated concern. "Did somebody leave you out in the rain and you rusted?"

Ellen thought the idea was hilarious. She looked to her mother to share the laugh. But there was that horrified expression again. The same one Marga had on her face after Ellen told her those neighborhood kids said she'd been dumped and left.

Why would this funny joke make Mommy so upset?

25

1964 – 1966

The Beatles' *A Hard Day's Night* was becoming one of the most popular movies in American theaters. Everyone wanted to see it. There was hardly ever an empty seat in the Tivoli Theater on the far eastern side of Richmond's Main Street. You never knew who you may see there.

It was one of many places in their hometown that the hunter, his grandson, Corky or his now teenaged daughter, and Ellen Test could have brushed shoulders. Ellen's family made annual trips to the eastern Indiana city to see relatives who still lived near Boston. In a town of thirty-five thousand with only one Main Street, one shopping mall, one library, one skate rink, two movie theaters and only a handful of popular restaurants, it would have been less likely that they never would have been at the same place at the same time.

But it's truly a small world. Both the Tests and Cordells had visited the World's Fair in New York City the summer before. There may have been any number of times Ellen was within a shoulder's brush of the sheriff, the hunters or the girl who'd grown up with a storybook image of a baby lying helpless at the roots of a tree in dense woods.

It's also true that the preteen may easily have shared glances with one or both of her biological parents. She may have unwittingly exchanged a nod or greeting with the very person who so callously dropped her to what that would-be murderer believed was the helpless infant's death.

Had those who cared about the tiny baby and continued to wonder about her seen the healthy and happy toddler, the growing child and now preteen on a Richmond street and been unaware? Did her would-be murderer see Ellen's reflection in a storefront window or whiz by her on roller skates? Maybe occupy a plush red upholstered seat behind her at the Tivoli movie theater?

It's something only God knows.

1963 trip to New York, which included
the World's Fair in New York City
(Front l-r: John Test, Kevin Shendler and Ellen Test;
back: Marlow, Ruth, and Marla Shendler,
and Ellen's parents Marga and Merwin Test)

Corky's wife Betty at the 1963 World's Fair in New York City

26

Ellen Test was excited. She was going to be a California girl, just like the sunshine-golden beauties the Beach Boys were singing about. Her father had been transferred to Corona, less than an hour's drive from Los Angeles. Marga and Merwin loaded up the station wagon, and with John, Ellen and the family dog, took in America the beautiful from coast to coast.

On their way, they stopped in Richmond for a visit with Ruth and Marlowe Shendler and their five children. Though the two families often took camping excursions or vacations together, such as their trip earlier that year to the World's Fair in New York City, this time the reunion was just a pause on their cross-country journey.

Ellen and her cousins Kim and Kevin took full advantage of their short time together. They played in the barn's hayloft, chased each other through fields near the Shendler's Boston farmhouse, skipped stones across the pond, and paid surprise visits to Kim and Kevin's grandparents down the road. Granner and Daddy Ray made Ellen feel so welcome and at-home she hated to leave. But it was California or bust.

The Tests had barely settled in their ranch-style home in Corona before Ellen decided it was definitely bust. Even though Mount Baldy was visible from their kitchen window, beautiful with its snow-covered cap, and there were rose bushes and fruit trees in their yard, Ellen was miserable.

Why was it always summer? She missed the changing seasons. And she missed her friends. She was the personification of despair sitting on the cement stoop in front of her new home: skirt sagging between her knees, toes inward, elbows propped on thighs and her cheeks resting morosely on fists.

"I hope it isn't all that bad."

Ellen raised her eyes without moving. A girl about her age, jump rope in hand, stood at the end of the walk. The young teen smiled. Ellen smiled back, lowering her hands.

"I knew it. I knew it couldn't be all that bad," the girl with the jump rope chuckled. "Wanna play?"

Her name was Debra Pierce and she lived two doors down from the Tests. Like Ellen, she was a couple inches taller than other girls their age. Slender with light brown hair and eyes, Debra had enviably long fingers. Perfect, since Ellen soon learned, she was a gifted piano player.

It wasn't long before Ellen and her new friend were inseparable. Debra's parents, Bill and June Pierce, became fast friends with the Tests. The two families often camped together. Merwin and Bill liked to hike while Marga and June sat in green canvas folding chairs and talked food. Both loved to bake.

"Mom likes to cook so much we never eat in a restaurant," Ellen told Debra one rainy day when they were passing time playing rummy inside their tent.

"Never? That's an exaggeration."

"Swear it's not. The only time we eat out is if we're traveling or Mom's in the hospital."

Marga's specialty was cupcakes. She baked dozens at a time while preparing for camping trips, then stored them in a chest freezer in the garage. If she ever noticed they disappeared at an alarming rate, she didn't let on. Maybe it was because she enjoyed listening to Ellen and Debra's muffled giggles coming from under the kitchen window.

June Pierce could have been a professional chef. She had rows of pans hanging from hooks on her kitchen wall. She was nothing if not organized. And that was a good thing because Debra's mother was often preoccupied.

Ellen and Debra came in from playing one afternoon to find a note propped against the napkin holder on the Pierce's maple dinette table. "Girls – there are pork chops in the pan on the stove."

There was no pan on the stove. Debra opened the Frigidaire. There was a plate of pork chops, but they were raw. Both girls fairly danced. This was their chance. "Let's fry them ourselves!"

Rising on her tiptoes, Ellen brought a copper skillet down from a wall hook. She might have frowned in disappointment, but giggled instead. She held the cookware at arm's length for Debra to see inside. Both girls doubled over, squealing raucous laughter.

Stuck to the inside of the pan were two crusty brown pork chops.

Debra Pierce Porter and Ellen Test Suey, all grown up,
with Bob Suey during a vacation in Kauai, Hawaii in 2014.

27

Marga Test handed the phone to Ellen. It was Sunday night, just past nine o'clock, when most Americans made their long distance calls. Rates decreased by half after nine on Sunday nights, so that's when the Tests and the Shendlers caught up on everything that mattered in the world.

"Uncle Marlowe?"

"It's me, sweetheart. What's up?"

Ellen cupped the mouthpiece with her hand and whispered into it. "Uncle Marlowe, if I ever had to go anywhere, if something happened to Mom and Dad and I had to live with anybody else, I'd call you to come pick me up."

"No you wouldn't," her uncle said. "Because I'd already be on my way to get you."

Ellen sighed relief. She loved her Uncle Marlowe second only to her father.

The next Sunday, uncle and niece missed their weekly chat. Ellen and John were at Pilgrim Pines Camp in the forested mountains outside Yucaipa, California. They'd gone with other kids and a few adults from their Presbyterian Church.

Ellen had hugged Debra goodbye that morning and promised to send postcards every day from church camp. The blank manila cards were already packed and stamped.

Even though her dearest friend didn't go along, Ellen loved the annual week-long inspirational camp. She looked forward to swimming in the pool, filled with icy cold water from mountain springs, and even found fun when she and the other eleven girls from her cabin were assigned a turn at KP duty.

Pilgrim Pines wasn't heavy on preaching, and didn't coax youngsters to come forward with altar calls. There were, however, daily devotions that were as natural as the regular morning calisthenics on the camp's rolling lawn. Counselors and chaperones bore silent testimony to Christ's message of love in interactions with their young charges.

Bouncing on the back seat of the church bus with every bump and pothole it hit on the winding two-lane road back to Corona, Ellen was considering what she'd heard during the week's devotions. She could see her reflection in the bus window's glass. Thinking about examples the adults at camp set that mirrored her own parents' Christian values, she began to ponder her own rocky behavior.

"That's when," she told Debra the next day, "I knew for sure that I need the Lord in my life."

Debra was smoothing a wig of bright yellow yarn glued on the gourd doll Ellen had presented her, a souvenir from one of Pilgrim Pines' craft days. "Watching pine trees pass by out the bus window made you think you need God in your life?"

"No, it was me looking back at me. I didn't want to come home as the same person I was when I left. Since I turned thirteen, I haven't been very proud of how I act sometimes. Debra, I think God makes a difference in a person's life. At least, it sure looks like it."

"What are you going to do? I mean, how do you do that – put the Lord in your life?"

"Well, I know I need to make a profession of faith in Jesus Christ. So, I'm going to go forward at church this Sunday.

"There was a picture in the devotional last week. Jesus is knocking at a door and there's no doorknob on the outside. It has to be opened from the inside. The door represents someone's heart and that person has to open it and invite Him in.

"That's what I'm going to do."

28

Ellen Test was fifteen when Merwin was transferred to the high desert town of China Lake, California. She was more miserable than she'd been when they moved to California in the first place. This time, they lived in military housing on the base. The area was dry, sterile and cold.

And then once again Debra came to her rescue. Her father was also transferred to China Lake. To add to that happy circumstance, Merwin and Marga had come up with a way to assure their daughter stayed away from the rumored drug and alcohol culture: the Tests bought Ellen her first horse. With her best friend Debra Pierce in the same town, and a new equestrian hobby, Ellen enjoyed happy and carefree high school years.

One high desert evening during her senior year, she walked into Albertson's Grocery where the brother of a friend from school worked. Two years older than she, Mike was blonde with blue eyes. He wore glasses that gave him a studious appearance that reminded her of her dad. So, when he asked her for a date right there in Albertson's, she didn't hesitate.

Mike and Ellen married in June, 1974, a year after she graduated high school. They set up housekeeping on an acre of land they bought so she could keep her horse close by. Mike worked nights at Albertson's and Ellen got a job as an instructional aide for the China Lake School District, working days. In 1976 when their son Christopher was born, Ellen took a leave of absence from the school.

She didn't work outside the home again until six months after daughter Traci was born in 1978 when she took a job as a bookkeeper for a propane company. The young family joined and became active in a Southern Baptist Church.

"This church sure is different from our Presbyterian church," Ellen told Debra.

The two women were having a Sunday night chat on the telephone. Debra had married John "Big Red" Porter, who called his wife's best friend Ellie Babe, and the girls were once again separated by a large span of California miles.

"Tell me about that another time. How are things at The Menagerie?"

Ellen laughed. With its horses, pony, four dogs, three cats, a turtle, a bird and a gaggle of feathered and noisy security guards commonly known as geese, her home had been dubbed by Marga "The Menagerie."

"We're all fine. Just got back from Richmond."

"Did you meet your Cousin Kim's wife?"

"Tammy? Yes, and guess what, she's adopted, too. From the same placement office, even. Her case worker was the same one as mine."

"Really. That's a coincidence."

"She's found her birthmother and wanted to know if I'd like her to try to find mine."

"What'd you say?"

"I said she could go ahead," Ellen said as if she didn't care one way or the other; it was just that unimportant to her. "She's done adoption searches for two other people and found their biological parents. She's pretty much proven herself to be what they call a 'Search Angel' so I guess we might know something pretty soon."

"Oh, she's looking now?" Debra sounded surprised.

"Well, Tammy's really afraid to hurt my mom's feelings. She said she just fell in love with Mom the moment she met her and wants my mother to like her, too. And I know Mom is afraid I might find my birth mom then leave her. It's not that I would do that, but I do want answers. Like, where and how did I get these scars?"

"Have you asked Marga?"

"Of course. You know that. I'll just have to find out another way, though, because she always says the same thing – 'sometimes adopted babies come that way'."

"How did she react when you told her you're looking for answers now?"

"She doesn't know. There's no reason to worry her. If Tammy finds anything, she'll let me know and then I'll decide what to do. Maybe I should start thinking about what I'm going to say now, though, because this Search Angel stuff is serious.

"Tammy is sure to find something out."

29

1981

Every chance she got, Tammy Shendler visited with Esther Kellner. A novelist and naturalist, Esther had befriended a lonely little girl whose adoption caseworker, Mary Hart, lived nearby. It was Mary who'd introduced the child to the writer. Growing up, Tammy had spent many happy afternoons in Esther's brown shingled house on Richmond's eastside.

Tammy was a young mother now who'd grown to be an ebullient woman with a contagious open smile and laugh. Though busy with her own home, taking care of husband Kim Shendler and their little son, she always found time to visit Esther, who maintained a type of hospital for ailing squirrels in her home. The two women would sit at Esther's kitchen table talking above the chatter of her furry patients kept in cages along the room's west wall.

After one cheerful visit in the spring of 1981, Tammy was driving back to her home thinking that if it hadn't been for Esther, she didn't know just how her life might have turned out. Haunted by an early trauma that involved the death of her baby sister, Tina,

Tammy was not only plagued by feeling unloved, but also often felt lonesome and afraid. Esther without fail helped her see the beauty in nature and her own life.

Today these thoughts had taken her miles and years away when she saw from her Volkswagen Rabbit Mary Hart sitting on her South 22nd Street porch. Her mind immediately went to Ellen and the years-ago promise to search for her birthparents. Maybe now was the time to start.

Tammy pulled to the curb, certain that Mary would be receptive to her inquiries on Ellen's behalf. Mary had always been compassionate to answer questions about why Tammy had been "taken away" from her birth mother. She climbed the cement steps to the seat Mrs. Hart, now eighty-one-years-old, patted invitingly.

Sitting next to each other on aluminum porch chairs, a vase of daffodils between them on a plant stand, the two made small talk. As always, when Tammy visited Mary, she'd been offered something refreshing to drink. Today, it was Tab with chipped ice. They sipped their drinks like two old friends with nothing to do but while away the afternoon.

Finally, Tammy asked Mary about a 1957 adoption, hoping the retired case worker might remember Merwin and Marga Test.

"I know the Tests quite well," Mary said. "They were thrilled to get Ellen. They used to send Christmas cards every year. Sometimes they still do. I'm glad to know that you and Ellen have met. Well, I guess you're cousins by marriage, now. Tell me, are her eyes still so very blue?"

"They are still blue," Tammy said, "but she doesn't know where she got them. I'm going to check records at the court house, but since I saw you today, I may as well ask: can Ellen see her welfare records?"

Mary hesitated. When she spoke, she seemed to choose her words carefully. "You know that adoption records are sealed."

"Ellen can see her birth records at the court house," Tammy said. "We'll go when she comes again next summer. But I was wondering if we can't see her welfare adoption file, too."

"I, uh, don't know. They're sealed. I don't even think a court order would do any good, Tammy. I believe those records have been, um . . . lost."

Mary purposefully lowered her eyes to her cat, curled into a neat ball in her lap. She'd been lightly running her palms over the soft brown fur, but now her hands were tightly clinched with fingers interlaced.

Perplexed, Tammy asked lightly, "Was Ellen dumped in the trash or something?"

Mary lifted her head, faltered as she glanced at Tammy, and then said quietly, "Something like that."

30
1982

Tammy's cheerfulness didn't ease the flutter of nerves she felt rising from her stomach through her heart and into her throat. It did, however, mask the trepidation she'd felt since Ellen had asked her earlier that day to take her to the Wayne County Courthouse. She'd not told Ellen what Mary Hart had said. It had been simply a hint, and the only one at that. Tammy had been unable to cajole the former caseworker into divulging anything more.

She and Ellen ascended the wide limestone steps in the center of the cavernous court house to the second floor County Recorder's office. Their footsteps echoed and mingled with deep-well voices from offices off the marbled hallways in the sprawling three-story building. It was a solemn place.

"Sometimes," Tammy said in a whisper, "they put cellophane tape over the biological parents' names on birth records of adopted babies. After a few years, the ink bleeds through and you can read the names. Let's keep our fingers crossed."

The assistant in the Recorders' office couldn't have been more pleasant. She readily wrote with a ballpoint pen on a square of scrap paper, "Birth records. September 18, 1955." She returned with a thick folder and directed the women to a large, square oak table against the wall.

"Now we'll find out who my mother was," Ellen said to Tammy.

Tammy frowned a warning, but it was too late. The assistant looked from one to the other then snatched up the files and without explanation walked briskly to her desk behind the forbidding black marble-topped counter.

"Let's go outside. I have another idea," Tammy said.

Once they were on the sidewalk, Ellen said, "I wanted to grab those files and run."

"She probably knew from what you said that yours was a case of adoption. Those records are sealed. Don't be discouraged, though. Let's go to the library to look at the birth announcements."

Tammy didn't mention Mary Hart's obscure clue. She knew too well the pain of knowing that you were an innocent victim of an unspeakable act, one at the hands of the very person who should love you most. She wasn't going to be the one to tell Ellen she was dumped in the trash. Or, ". . . something like that."

There might be a newspaper article around Ellen's birthday, Tammy reasoned, that would give an account of an abandoned baby. But she was going to let Ellen find it for herself.

They walked across the street to Morrisson-Reeves Library to look at microfiche newspaper articles. "It hurts my eyes to see those pages whir by," Tammy explained convincingly. "I'll run get more tapes for you when you're ready, and sit here with you. But you do the reading."

Tammy, who'd used the microfiche machines many times in her searches, threaded the first reel through the projector. They started with a tape that began a few days before what Ellen believed to be her birthdate: September 18, 1955. Ellen sat at the machine and began to slowly turn the handle to pull the film from the left reel through the projector and wind it onto the right-hand reel. The pages flashed past on the monitor but could still be seen without Ellen pausing to closely read every page. She stopped motion only when she saw the headline "For the Record" in each edition.

There was nothing that might link Ellen with any of the births she saw listed. She found it fascinating, though, to view old, dramatic headlines and vintage advertisements featuring ridiculously low prices. She began to stop the reels at each front page, theater listings – "Look how handsome James Dean was in 'Rebel Without a Cause" – and the many advertisement pages.

Eventually she stopped the reel at the front page of the September 23, 1955 edition. It was just a headline. No photograph. The article itself was brief. But it was shocking.

As she read the headline aloud, Ellen didn't notice that Tammy stiffened. "Hunters Find New-Born Tot Lying in Woods."

Her eyes trained on the monitor, Ellen said, "How sad. It says hunters found it on the edge of woods. Oh, my, it says the baby had been there twelve to twenty-four hours. And it wasn't born in a hospital. That poor little thing."

Tammy's breath caught. She said nothing.

Ellen began turning the reel again, pausing at the movies, the ads, the succinct clerk, courts, and hospital records. Then a later edition came into view. This time, a front-page headline over a photo of a nurse holding a baby announced in bold font, "Tiny Baby Girl Found in Woods at Boston."

"At least she lived," Ellen said. She began to read the story then stopped short.

"This could be me! This baby might be me!"

Tears formed pools in Tammy's eyes. "Yes, it could be you."

31

Clutching copies of the 1955 microfiche articles about the newborn baby found in the woods, Ellen sat in an overstuffed chair in Tammy's family room. "All we have to go on is what Mrs. Hart said. Where do we go from here?"

"We start making phone calls," Tammy said.

Armed with only the names of people mentioned in the two articles, they flipped pages in the phone book and dialed General Telephone operators for numbers. There were no listings for a Clay Smith or David Hickman. Jenny Parrish, the nurse pictured holding the baby who may be Ellen, was almost impossible to find. Eventually, someone from Reid Hospital remembered her and thought maybe she'd moved to nearby Dayton, or some other town in eastern Ohio.

Tammy was driven. Using skills she'd honed over the past few years of searching for birthparents, she made call after call until she found the retired nurse. Dialing the number, she handed the phone to Ellen. Only a few moments later, Ellen replaced the receiver in its cradle.

"She was very vague. Wonder why. So what now?"

"I talked to Corky Cordell's secretary about my case because he was sheriff then, too," Tammy said. "Maybe she can tell us something about you . . . this baby."

The next day they were sitting beside Pauline Starr's hospital bed in Oak Ridge Nursing Home. The room was bright, with a large window that opened to a courtyard in the middle of the single-story red brick building. A still life oil painting hung on the wall opposite Pauline's bed where she could see it above her mother's bureau. She'd been unable to bring more than just a few belongings with her when she moved permanently to the nursing facility, so she'd chosen carefully.

It didn't take a lot of discernment to realize that Pauline was very frail. Her little body was like a fragile skeleton. She was kept warm from head to toe by a hand-sewn quilt she'd brought from home. But her smile was wide, her eyes quick.

Ellen got right to the point. "Miss Starr, do you remember a little baby that was found in woods by a hunter?"

"Oh, I do," Pauline said. "She was such a pretty little thing. When they brought her to the office to let us see her before she was adopted, I thought she looked like a little doll baby. She had on the sweetest blue dotted Swiss dress that we'd . . ."

Though Pauline continued speaking, Ellen didn't hear anything more. Buzzing in her ears was as loud as if they'd been invaded by a swarm of bees. Tammy and Pauline appeared to be swallowed by a telescoping fog as her vision narrowed to nothing but the recollection of a vintage doll her mother kept in her Arizona home. Marga had preserved the dress worn by her daughter the first time Ellen had been placed in her arms.

The doll tenderly displayed in her parents' antique oak curio cabinet was dressed in that faded but prized blue dotted Swiss dress.

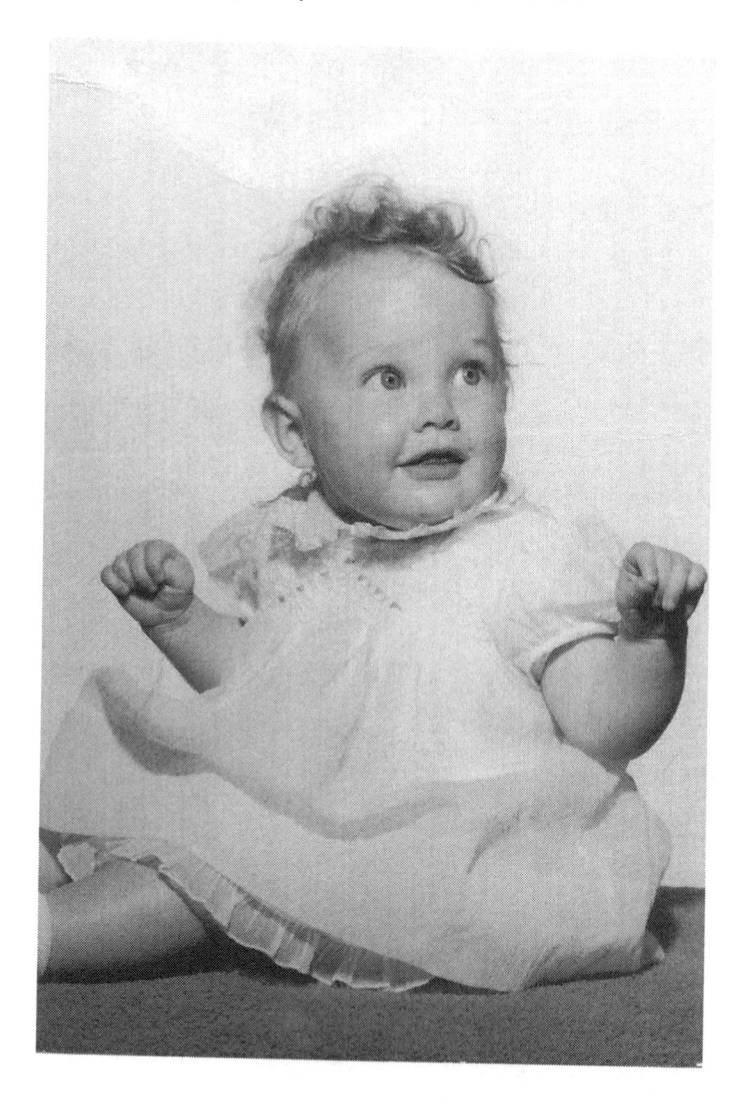

Ellen wearing the blue dotted Swiss dress bought for her by sheriff's department staff

32

Pauline instructed Tammy to pour a glass of water from a plastic pitcher on her nightstand.

"I'm sorry," Ellen said, sipping the iced water. She swallowed, gulped a breath then blurted, "What a shock!"

She explained about the doll and the validating dress it wore. "Until yesterday I didn't know anything about an abandoned baby. And today – just now – I know for certain that it's me."

Her left hand caressed the oval scar on her neck. "Do you know how I got this? Can you tell me anything about my parents?"

"Why, honey," Pauline asked wonderingly, "didn't they tell you?"

Who did she mean? Marga and Merwin? The Welfare Department? Law enforcement authorities? Ellen shook her head. No one had told her anything.

Pauline ignored the first question, but said with confidence, "You came from influential people from Ohio."

Tammy urged Pauline to continue, but the former secretary appeared to have realized she may have said too much.

Ellen felt that her brain couldn't take in anything more anyway. It was as if her mind were a thin latex balloon filled to bursting. Just the knowledge that she had been purposely left to die when she was just days old was overwhelming. She couldn't quite process the additional information that the person who left a helpless baby in cold wet woods was influential and perhaps wealthy. Or that the horrible person was quite possibly her biological parent. She could hardly think.

That evening she called the former sheriff. "Mr. Cordell?"

"Oh," he pretended to chide with a smile in his voice, "I'm Corky."

Ellen sighed with relief. "Corky, do you remember the baby found in the woods twenty-seven years ago? I'm that baby."

"I know who you are."

He proved his assertion. "I've been following you all your life. You're married, live in California and have two children."

Typical of many politicians, it could be that he wanted her to feel he knew her. Maybe Pauline had called to let him know about Ellen's visit. It could have been Mary Hart who'd tipped him off a few years earlier that Tammy was asking questions.

Had he really been keeping track of her since 1955? It's possible that Mary Hart had shared Christmas cards all along without letting him know the Test name or home. Maybe there had been a compassionate reason he hadn't let on that he always knew where Ellen was.

It could be that he was being truthful with Ellen at that moment and still have been truthful with his daughter for twenty-seven years. While recounting, dozens of times over those years, the story of the hunter who'd found a newborn baby under a tree, he'd never failed to wistfully muse, "I wonder where she is now. I hope she's had a good life."

Ellen believes he always knew her whereabouts. Corky's daughter Mary Ellen is positive he didn't.

Either way, Ellen was about to get some answers.

Psalm 32:8 – *I will guide you along the best pathway for your life. I will advise you and watch over you.*

I felt that God was giving me bits and pieces of my story. I needed to digest it slowly. God knew when the right time was to give me another piece of the puzzle.

Ellen Suey

33

It had never occurred to Ellen that she'd had any other name than the one her parents had given her. So she was taken aback when Corky greeted her, four-year-old Traci, and Tammy at the front door of his modest west side home the next morning. "Rose Wayne!"

He was so obviously happy to see her, with his wide grin and dancing blue eyes, that Ellen didn't correct him. Instead she took his outstretched hand then turned to introduce her cousin-in-law.

"Aw, Tammy and I are old friends," the former sheriff said.

The three visitors sat in the Cordells' family room, Corky's wife, Betty, sitting just behind him near the kitchen. They'd barely sat down before Corky explained with pride to Ellen how he'd named her at Reid Hospital the day after she'd been found. He said that Ann had been added later; he wasn't sure if by nurses or welfare workers. But to him, she was always Rose Wayne.

Corky didn't ask how she'd discovered that she was the baby left in the woods, a hint that perhaps Pauline had given him a call the day before. His former secretary's mind and heart must have been reeling after realizing Ellen hadn't known her story until she had inadvertently divulged the secret by describing to the young woman the little dress that proved her identity.

Barely pausing after explaining how he'd come up with her original name, Corky's face changed to seriousness. "You know, I wanted to adopt you."

No, she didn't know that. Another surprise. How might her life have been different? Would she have been called Rose or Roseann since the Cordells already had a daughter named Mary Ellen? And what about her own parents? *They love me so much,* she was thinking, saddened by the thought of imaginary years of the Tests without their daughter.

"But the Welfare Department wouldn't let me," he was saying as if still disappointed by their decision. "You had to be adopted by a family living out-of-state because there was so much notoriety about how you were found. There was news coverage all over, even television and radio. It was even in Cincinnati papers and their T.V. evening news."

"Speaking of Cincinnati," Ellen said, "were my biological parents influential people from Ohio?"

Corky's face collapsed from jolly round-cheeks to uncharacteristic anger. "That's a lie! Who told you that?"

"Pauline, your secretary," Ellen managed.

His face relaxed. "Oh, well, you can't pay any attention to what she says. She's a sweet old lady and doesn't remember things very well anymore."

Ellen thought of the secretary's precise recollection of the little dress, but didn't press. "Corky, do you know how I got these scars?"

"Well, that's how we could judge how old you were. When you were found, maggots had already gotten into the wounds. They had a hard time removing them at the hospital."

Ellen, her mouth grimacing downward in disgust, involuntarily felt with her fingertips the slick, taut skin below her jaw. "Maggots?"

Corky nodded as if he didn't realize that she'd been unaware of the appalling scope of her injuries.

"Cork!" his wife scolded. Though little Traci had fallen asleep and hadn't heard the disturbing news, the old sheriff's wife was keenly aware that the information was an obvious shock to Ellen.

Corky raised his eyebrows in mock injury as if he'd been falsely accused. He smiled an apology at Ellen. "It's a miracle you lived, young'un. If it hadn't been for those . . . uh, well, you know, their work on your umbilical cord might have saved your life. It hadn't been tied and was bleeding."

"It hadn't been tied?"

"That's how we knew you weren't born in a hospital. Those . . . uh, gave us about the only clues we had. Their size and advanced burrowing into your skin gave us evidence that you were at least two days old and probably more when you were found. And, that you were born somewhere where there were lots of flies and you'd been left laying for several days. What we didn't know was how long you were in the woods. We guessed that by how wet the towel was."

"What towel?"

"You were only wrapped in a towel and it was soaking wet from all the rain we'd had that night and morning. If that hunter hadn't found you when he did, you probably wouldn't have lived much longer. Even then, everybody must have been afraid to cover you with one of their coats. To think you survived at all is a miracle.

"You're a miracle."

Psalm 66:5 - *Come and see what our God has done. What awesome miracles He performs for people.*

Listening to Corky talk that day, I realized the miracle God had performed in my life.

Ellen Suey

34

The Cordells' daughter never knocked. Their visits to each other's Richmond homes were so frequent and casual that they just walked right in. Usually when Mary Ellen came into her parents' home, she found them watching television. Her mother was sometimes in the kitchen, her father in his "rock room" where he made jewelry. There were never overt greetings or the fanfare of receiving a visitor.

Today, though, her dad met her at the door. He'd heard her come into the driveway so he was waiting with an outstretched hand, a slip of paper in his fist. A name, address and phone number were written in blue ink.

"Guess who was here today?!"

His daughter looked from the paper to his elated face. Before she could guess, he joyfully announced as if his visitor had been President Ronald Reagan himself, "Rose Wayne!"

"Rose Wayne! Why didn't you call me?"

Corky Cordell putting on a puppet show for granddaughter Emily Donat (1982)

35

There was so much to think about. Back in California, Ellen pondered the idea that there was no doubt she should not have survived those first few days of life. She knew from her own children, Christopher and Traci, how much attention newborns require. How could an infant survive without any food or water? Bleeding and infested by parasites, left in a wilderness where she knew in Indiana wild pigs, coyotes, and even wolves were common? And the rain! That relentless, bone-chilling rain.

"But for the grace of God," she told Debra Pierce Porter over the phone, "I would surely have died."

"He sent those hunters to the right place at the right time, that's for sure."

"I thought when Tammy took me to the courthouse and then the library I'd find my birth parents. I sure never expected to discover anything like this."

"Are you going to try to find the hunters? And your bio parents?"

"Yes and yes. Tammy's following up on some leads. The sheriff told us there were later newspaper stories, so she's going back to the library to find those, then contact people whose names are mentioned. If we'd looked just a little further that day, we'd have seen what they named me at the hospital and . . ."

"What was it?"

"Roseann Wayne."

"I like it. But I like Ellen better. But you were going to say something else."

"I was just going to say that now I want to find the picture that shows Mother holding me the day they got me."

"You sure did get some great parents."

"Debra, I've been thinking a lot about that. God chose perfect parents for me. I wonder if they know about all this. I don't want to ask them over the phone. I'm going to Arizona, but first I have something else to do.

"When I realized what happened to me as a baby, I started thinking how much the Lord's done for me. I feel the need to rededicate my life to the Lord and be baptized again."

36

It wasn't yet sunrise. Ellen sat at her parents' Sun City, Arizona kitchen table. Ready for another hot day in the city her parents had chosen for their retirement, she was already dressed in shorts and sandals. She rested her cheek against her hand, elbow on the table as she watched her mother pour two steaming cups of Folgers. Just as Marga brought the coffee to the table, Merwin sauntered in. He, too, was dressed for the day. Everyone else was still asleep, including Christopher and Traci.

"Mom, Dad," Ellen said, fiddling with the handle of her cup, "I want to tell you about my trip to Aunt Ruth's."

Merwin joined his wife and daughter at the table. He quietly spooned sugar and powdered creamer into his cup then absently stirred, waiting. The knot in his stomach told him that this might be the day they'd been dreading. Yet, it might be the day they'd also been anticipating. Fearing the inevitable; ready for the awful suspense to at last be over.

"I found out about what happened before you adopted me."

Ellen not only heard audible relief but could also feel it from the other side of the table. She looked up from the creamy clouds dissipating into her coffee. Her parents were smiling, the constricting binds of their terrible secret at last loosed. She could almost see them exhale tight breaths that had been held far too long.

Marga said, "I am so relieved we didn't have to tell you. I thought we should when you turned eighteen, but your father thought it was such a horrific ordeal that he was afraid it would hurt you."

"What do you know and who told you?" asked Merwin.

Ellen told them everything she'd read in the microfiche articles, also relieved that her parents already knew she'd been left to die. She told them how Pauline Starr had verified her suspicions that she was the baby in the microfiche articles by inadvertently mentioning the dotted Swiss dress, and the additional details provided by Corky Cordell.

"Did Corky tell you about the lab results on the towel?"

"No. He didn't mention testing. Do you know what they were?"

"There's not much," her father said. "The towel was sent to the Indiana State Police laboratory. There was a faint laundry mark from Cincinnati's Gibson Hotel."

"Cincinnati? A hotel?"

"A luxury hotel near the Ohio River. But the towel was rather threadbare, not a new one that a four-star hotel like that would still be using."

"Anything else?" asked Ellen.

Her parents looked at each other. "Two hairs. One from a human; pubic. The other from a dog."

"A dog? Do you think a dog might have kept me warm and safe while I was in the woods?"

Her voice trailed off as she had an enlightening thought: perhaps that's why she has such a deep love of animals, particularly canines.

"Well, we don't know that," her father said. "It's possible. We really don't know anything more."

"So, you don't have any idea who may have left me there?"

Marga reached across the table to caress her daughter's hand. "We don't. Even if we did, we'd never speak ill of your birth parents. We've forgiven them. If it weren't for them, we wouldn't have you. Every year on your birthday, and every mothers' day I pray for the woman who gave birth to you. It's my hope, Ellen, that she may someday make a confession and find peace. Hopefully before her deathbed."

Her parents both audibly sighed as if to signal the end of not only their story but also their trial. Their shoulders sagged, not from weight but from the lifting of the heavy burden they'd carried for twenty-seven years.

"I don't think anyone else would be so charitable," Ellen later told Debra. "I was a fortunate little girl to have been placed in their arms to raise."

Marga and Merwin Test outside their Arizona home (circa 1996)

Matthew 6:14-15 – *For if you forgive others for their transgressions, your heavenly Father will also forgive you. But if you do not forgive others, then your Father will not forgive your transgressions.*

It was amazing and just part of God's plan for me to be able to start pulling my puzzle together.

God showed me once again how much love and compassion my folks had for me. They took a child like me and raised her as their own, unconditionally.

My folks showed me once again about forgiveness. They never held any anger towards the person or persons who left me to die. They prayed for them.

If God can forgive us then we need to step up and do the same.

Ellen Suey

37

1983 – 1987

Ellen held the letter in her right hand, its torn envelope dangling from her left. She'd had high hopes that perhaps the deputy sheriff who'd taken her to the hospital that awful evening in 1955 could shed some light on the who-and-why mysteries. She already knew the where. The questions that now troubled her were who would leave her in that desolate spot, and what were the circumstances?

But Dale Defibaugh had written a disappointingly brief letter. The words that mattered most to Ellen were near his signature. "I only played a small part."

Another dead end. She was running out of avenues to explore. It seemed that Clay Smith and his grandson had simply vanished. Despite several attempts to find the two hunters, Ellen was beginning to think she would never find them. Besides, she had other things on her mind.

Mike was attentive and courteous the first nine years of their marriage. The physical and emotional abuse began gradually. Ellen knew God hates divorce, but she also understood that abuse was an exception as part of His mercy and grace.

Putting aside Dale's letter, Ellen turned her attention to more immediate matters. She was determined to seek employment that would support her and the kids if she needed to leave her marriage.

It didn't take her long to find work as an administrative assistant with the Department of Defense. By 1985, the decision was made to end her marriage to Mike.

Two years later, Ellen transferred to Corona and moved to Riverside, California with her two children. Her office was on the same military base where her father had worked when they first came to California, so she felt right at home. And just as it hadn't been long before she'd found a friend in Debra Porter, Ellen soon found several friends from the office who liked to take walks and chat during lunch hours.

"We'll be fine," she told Debra during one of their long-distance calls.

Sometimes months passed between their phone chats, but the friends always started up again as if they'd talked only the day before. "Chris and Traci love their school. And I couldn't be happier at work. I think I'm even losing a few pounds walking every day."

"How's the investigation going? Anything new?"

"No," Ellen sighed. "Either nobody knows anything, or they're not talking. It's like there's a big secret or something."

"You must be so frustrated."

"Well, I could be. But maybe I should just be resigned to the fact that I'll have to wait to see the Lord face to face to get all the answers I need."

Maybe it was just saying it out loud, but with that, Ellen handed her burden to God. He had saved her thirty years ago, had placed her in a Christian home and revealed Himself to her in a mighty way just three years before. She was trusting Him with every aspect of her life now. There was no reason, in light of His presence and power that she couldn't trust that on one bright morning He would reveal all that was now hidden from her.

38

1995 – 1998

She wasn't forty in her heart. In fact, the way she was feeling today, Ellen Test felt as if she really were the quintessential young and beautifully tanned California girl. She was by all internal indications a mere teenager, sitting with the guy she was about to marry on the sandy shore of Newport Beach near her Riverside home. Their bare toes kneaded the sand as they talked above the crashing of waves that crawled toward them then rushed back to the Pacific.

Bob Suey, an electrical engineer for the Department of Defense, had been a part of the group of co-workers who hiked noontimes around the base perimeter. Affable but quiet, Bob was easy to talk to. The two soon became walking buddies then date mates. He was a brave guy, Ellen told Debra after he proposed, to take on a strong-willed woman with two teenagers.

"He proved it," Ellen laughed after she'd given her friend the news of her engagement. "He taught Traci to drive. Even parallel parking!"

She wanted no secrets between them. Bob already knew that Ellen had been briefly married a second time following her divorce from Mike. This sunny day, on the beach with nothing but shorebirds as witnesses, she felt that it was the right place and time to tell him about the baby left to die in the woods. And, though he'd never asked, to explain her scars.

Ellen pressed her feet into the sand, digging first her heels into the grit, then her toes. She didn't look at Bob, though she clutched his hand as if she could borrow his strength. He didn't say anything, just listened attentively.

She told him about being cruelly left to die, being found by two squirrel hunters, the former secretary's astonishing confirmation of her suspicions, and the sheriff's equally shocking revelations the next day. Pausing only when swallowing or taking in a deep breath of salt air, Ellen recalled Corky Cordell's explanation of her wounds, her parents' astounding forgiveness, and her own fruitless search for answers.

"But for the past ten years or so," she finished, "I've put it all in God's hands."

Bob unwound his fingers from hers and took her hand with his other. Pulling her close he kissed her temple. "I didn't think I could love you any more than I already did."

A few months later, on May 27, the two sealed their wedding vows with a kiss in a quaint chapel on the San Pedro pier.

Ellen and Bob Suey on their wedding day with her parents, his mother and grandmother

39

Life with Bob Suey was as sweet as honey. He proved to be the perfect father for two teenagers who'd inherited their mother's passion for animals.

One day while mowing a neighbor's yard, Christopher found a baby kitten abandoned, hungry, and afraid. When he brought the poor mewing kitty home, he'd not entertained a smidgen of a thought that Bob might object. Living in a home with so much love was just that easy.

A year and a half later, in the fall of 1996, Merwin Test passed away after a short battle with an aggressive form of cancer. Marga decided to remain in Sun City, Arizona, doing the best she could to cope with being alone for the first time in nearly half a century. Bob and Ellen Suey couldn't leave their jobs or take their teenagers out of school, so they drove five and a half hours every month to visit Ellen's mother for the weekend.

Ellen had promised her father shortly before his death that she would take good care of her mother. He'd brought the subject up by asking her if she'd ridden with Marga lately. Ellen had answered, "Do I look crazy?"

She relayed the story to Bob on one of their trips to Sun City. "He laughed until I had tears in my eyes."

Their laughter fell to chuckles. Bob squeezed Ellen's hand in her lap. They were quiet, contentedly watching the California hardscape become Arizona desert, beautiful with its saguaro cacti.

"Bob, for a long time I felt that God didn't want me to look for the hunters or my biological parents anymore. But since we've been married, I've begun to think that it might be His timing for me to begin again. The hunter is probably passed away by now, but I have a name for his grandson and one of the deputies. It's like, if I can find some kind of closure on these questions, I can move on with my life."

"I think you should, then." Bob took his eyes from the highway to glance a reassuring smile in Ellen's direction. "What can I do to help?"

"Pray."

In the following weeks, Ellen found addresses for a David Hickman in Richmond, Indiana and Julian Benner in Boston, Indiana. She wrote to both, telling them who she was and her background, including that she'd been adopted by Merwin and Marga Test who'd raised her in California but had retired to Arizona. She told Mr. Benner that he might remember her grandfather, a veterinarian from Cambridge City, Indiana.

She received a letter from Mr. Hickman, but it was merely a courtesy response to inform her that he was not the man who'd found the baby. He added that he didn't know who or where that man was.

A notecard arrived a few days later from Meta Jane Benner, Julian's widow. Ellen's heart sank as she read the brief message. Though she'd often heard her husband talk about the baby found in the woods, Meta herself knew nothing about it.

"Bob," Ellen said, waving the card in defeat. "I think God is telling me that this isn't His timing after all. I'm sure He'll tell me when it's time, if it ever is in this life."

She remembered and respected that conviction during annual trips to visit her cousin, Kevin Shendler. He lived on a quiet country road just south of Richmond, near Boston. During morning walks, she and Bob often passed the home of former Wayne County Sheriff John Catey.

Inevitably, she said the same thing, year after year. "I'd like to go knock on his door to see if he can help me find anything out, but I just don't think it's God's timing. So I won't."

Sheriff John Catey with former sheriffs
Mac McCann and Corky Cordell (1976)

40
2001

A tiny fist curled around Ellen's index finger. Her first grandchild was cradled comfortably in the crook of her right arm. He was the first of her family to be nestled there since she'd learned of her brutal abandonment as an infant.

Christopher Joe had been born May 12, 2001 to Ellen's son Chris and his wife Ninive. They had just brought him home from the hospital and at last Ellen held the tiny bundle, just days old.

She leaned her face close to her grandson's thick dark hair and breathed in his sweet, warm newborn smell; the unmistakable heaven-scent that lingers but for a few days. Ellen held that long deep breath, her eyes closed, before exhaling through her smiling mouth along with an audible sigh; tangible evidence of profound joy.

"How," she wondered to herself as she kissed her grandson's forehead, warm and covered with wisps of silky down, "could anyone drop a sweet and innocent child of God over a barbed wire fence then leave it to die? How could anything this delicate and small survive for over three days without food or shelter? It was only by God's mercy that as those men looked on as I suffered a final hour in that cold rain before help arrived, that I am here to hold this sweet, sweet baby in my arms today."

She didn't want to think about that. It was her thought every time she'd held a baby since that day in Pauline Starr's room. Today she wanted only happy thoughts.

Aloud she said, "It's going to be confusing to call him Chris, too. I'm going to come up with my own name for him."

Nin bent to take her son. Ellen wiped a tear from her cheek with the back of her hand. She whispered a prayer of thanksgiving, still aware that but for the grace of God, she would not have survived to be the age of the baby now nuzzling his mother's neck. She said, "Thank You, Lord, for this boy. This perfect boy. Thank You, thank You."

Ellen's daughter-in-law was also grateful for her perfect son. She wasn't, however, at all sure that all was perfect with the baby they'd all begun to call Bubba. His breathing seemed labored and his color was pale. Nin took him to the doctor nearly every other week. The young mother felt helpless against the admonishments of the doctor. "You're just a worry wart," he'd say, dismissing not only Nin's concern but also the physical evidence before him.

Though she wanted to, Nin couldn't take Bubba to a different doctor for a second opinion because the closest hospital was Kaiser Permanente Riverside Medical Center, which chose physicians for their patients. She had no choice but to take the baby to the same physician time after time. She could, however, take along an advocate; one she knew would take a stand against an apathetic doctor.

41

"Ellen," Nin said into her kitchen telephone's receiver, clasped between her shoulder and ear as she held her fussy two-month-old, "can you go with me to the doctor this afternoon? I just know there is something wrong with Bubba. That doctor won't listen to me, but I'll bet he'll listen to you."

Ellen glanced at the pile of papers in her in-box. "Sure. Just let me give my boss a heads up. I'll be right over."

Apathy is no respecter of persons, however. As Ellen strapped her grandson into his car seat following the rushed office visit, she muttered, "I am not impressed with that guy at all."

Six months later, though, she was back with Nin and little Bubba to see the same physician. This time, Bob accompanied them. The doctor took a brief look at the wan baby struggling for breath and stated as if he'd not dismissed these symptoms many times before, "This baby needs to see a pediatrician."

"What?" Ellen declared incredulously. "Aren't you a pediatrician?"

His face a study of arrogance, the doctor declared in a tone that clearly implied that she should have known better, "This is a family practice."

Again, a physician was assigned by Kaiser. The pediatrician recognized immediately that Bubba was in trouble and had him admitted to the hospital. Kaiser Permanente Riverside Medical Center, however, lacked the technical support to run the necessary tests to correctly diagnose the baby's condition. So, tiny Bubba, with his mother beside him, took his first ambulance ride to Kaiser Permanente Fontana Medical Center.

He wasn't there long, however. Following a battery of tests, Ellen and her family were given the news they'd feared.

"Christopher has a condition called Transposition of the Great Arteries," the Fontana physician informed them as if it were a matter of course.

"What does that mean?" Nin asked.

"Basically," the doctor sighed, "the left artery isn't connected to the heart and the right side is doing all the work. We'll need to send this little guy to either Sunset in Los Angeles or Loma Linda for surgery."

Surgery! Ellen caught her breath. Bubba wasn't yet a year old. Her mind was a whirling blur. Loma Linda was closer; only fifteen minutes away from Riverside. She knew her way around it better. But before she could say anything, the decision was made. Bubba would take his second ambulance ride to Kaiser Permanente Los Angeles Medical Center. This time, however, he would be going alone.

Even though his mother had been permitted to ride in the ambulance from the first Kaiser Medical Center to this one, the staff at Kaiser Permanente Fontana Medical Center, citing insurance regulations, refused to allow Nin to ride in the ambulance to the Kaiser location on Sunset Boulevard, more than an hour away.

As Bubba was taken from Nin's arms, he screamed. His little arms stretched toward Nin and his hungry hands beseeched her. Crying large tears that coursed his cheeks, he was taken by a stranger to the waiting ambulance.

By the time the family reached their car in the Fontana hospital's parking lot, the ambulance was well on its way to Los Angeles. Unable to follow the emergency vehicle, Bubba's parents and grandparents followed a map and road signs. In a time before GPS, they had no real idea of where they were going. Ellen prayed constantly; for Bubba, his parents, the surgeon, and that they would safely arrive at a strange hospital in a city not known for easy traffic.

When they finally arrived at the Los Angeles hospital and found their way to the pediatric unit, they could hear Bubba's screams. Nin rushed to her baby and took him from an obviously flustered nurse.

"Good," the nurse said. "You're finally here. He's been screaming and screaming."

It may have been the mounting stress or the trouble finding the hospital, but most probably it was the sight of her precious grandson finally quieting in the arms of his mother that broke Ellen's patience. She couldn't remain silent. "If Mom had been allowed to ride with him, this wouldn't have happened."

Kaiser Permanente Los Angeles Medical Center was more accommodating after Bubba was admitted. Surgery was scheduled to be performed in just a few days. Nin was allowed to stay in his room, though the only place to sleep was on the floor beside his crib.

Bubba was home in less than a week to await surgery. Ellen marveled to Bob, "God was working on our boy!"

42

At home in Riverside, Ellen prayed throughout the long night before her grandson's scheduled operation. She asked for God's will and mercy. She asked for the Great Physician to be in control of the open-heart surgery, to heal his tiny heart, to guide the surgeons' hands. She prayed for wisdom of the staff at not only this, but all Kaiser medical centers.

And then she got the call.

Just before sunrise, Ellen and Bob were stepping from their Riverside home to head to Los Angeles when their phone rang. It was Chris. The planned surgery had been cancelled and the hospital was sending Bubba home. No, he told his incredulous mother, Bubba was not better.

"What's changed?" Ellen asked.

"When I changed jobs, my insurance changed. I'm using COBRA until my new insurance kicks in. Kaiser said they don't want to mess with the two insurances – the new one and COBRA – said we'll just have to figure it out for ourselves."

Chris paused. "That's not all. We'll have to get a new pediatrician, too."

Devastated, Ellen replaced the receiver. They were starting from Point A again. It seemed she'd lived this before: a helpless infant's life in the selfish hands of someone who cared more about convenience than the child's survival. Together, she and Bob cried their frustration and fear.

"Call on Romans 8:28," Bob said. "God has intended this for good. Let's keep praying."

Chris and Nin brought their seriously ill baby home. They thought they had no choice but to care for Bubba themselves until they could find a pediatrician and get their insurance straightened out. A week later, however, the baby was again laboring to breathe. His shallow gasps were alarming. Chris and Nin rushed him to a hospital not far from their home. Bob and Ellen met them there.

The emergency room staff at Riverside Community Hospital saw immediately that the baby was in distress. Bubba took his third ambulance ride in as many weeks to Loma Linda University Hospital, which had no problem dealing with complicated insurance policies.

"Thank You, Lord!" Ellen sighed with relief. Through tears of gratitude she looked at her husband. "Bob, this is where we wanted to go in the first place. 'All things happen for good . . .' God is watching over our sweet guy."

Bubba was evaluated at Loma Linda University Hospital where it was determined that though he had but a twenty percent chance of surviving open-heart surgery, that was the only option for the desperately ill six-month-old. Nin was able to stay with her baby, sometimes sleeping in chairs in his hospital nursery, until his surgery a week later.

It was answered prayer that Bubba, breathing normally and flush with color, was home just days later.

Ecclesiastes 3:1 – *To everything there is a season, and a time to every purpose under the heaven*

This situation just shows us how God can take an ugly situation and turn it around for good.

God was showing us that He does things in His time, He doesn't need our help. Prayers are always welcome.

This showed me that prayer is the most powerful tool we have. We wanted Bubba to go to Loma Linda in the first place. God said, "Wait." Then he said, "Go."

I've told Bubba's story so many times, and how God brought us what we needed in His time, not ours. I've told people to pray; pray without ceasing.

Ellen Suey

43
2003

Corky Cordell had been gravely ill, hospitalized in Indianapolis for several weeks. Though he'd been sleeping or largely unresponsive for several days, this sunny April morning he was alert. His daughter was surprised. Just the day before he'd opened his azure blue eyes from a deep sleep and focused intently on hers.

"I *love* you, Grandma," he'd said.

She'd laughed but immediately regretted it. She should have said, even if he may have thought it was his own mother's gentle mother answering him, "I love you, too." But he'd already closed his eyes.

Although he had seemed alert on previous days, he usually wasn't what Mary Ellen would deem to be 'present.' Once in a while he could be coaxed to conscious reality. In hopes that he would come back to her, she would often talk to him about what was going on in the world, tell him gossip from Richmond, plan things to do when he was well enough to leave the hospital.

One warm spring day she'd said, talking about a decades-long annual chore at their weekend Ohio River home, "It'll be time to put the dock in soon."

Her father replied as if waking from a dream, "Okay. I'll go get my tools."

Today, April 3, Mary Ellen was thankful that he was sitting up in his hospital bed smiling and talking coherently. There was no hint of the man who'd just the day before mistaken her for his beloved grandmother. His conversations with her and his wife Betty were clear and connected. Perhaps, his daughter thought, he was beginning to recover.

Just after lunch, she bent and kissed his cheek. "Bye, Dad."

Her mother would stay the rest of the afternoon, as she did every day, before returning to the Donats' home for the night.

As she walked from his room, Mary Ellen heard him call, "Have fun!"

It was the last thing he said to her. Good advice. Typical of him.

The next day, April 4, it rained. Mary Ellen decided that because she'd just washed her car she would wait to visit her father until the next day when the forecast called for sunny weather. They'd just finished supper and Mary Ellen was reading while her husband and mother watched a baseball game when the phone rang. Somehow – could it be possible? – this larger-than-life man had passed away.

That night and the next morning Mary Ellen was troubled because she had believed that they were so close that she would automatically know when her father passed from this life to the next; that he would reassure her that he was in God's glory. She was contemplating this when for no apparent reason a heart-shaped box, one among several, suddenly fell from a shelf, its only content spilling to the floor. She bent to pick up a necklace her father had made, a tiger eye stone in the center of a filigree cross.

The night of Corky's funeral calling was chilly and wet. Yet the stream of people paying their respects was constant for more than four hours. The queue stretched far beyond the sidewalk in front of Stegall-Berheide-Orr Funeral Home, visitors sharing umbrellas and tales. Several came from miles away. One, a former Palladium Item reporter who now wrote for the Chicago Tribune, had made the long drive to Richmond.

Corky's son-in-law Tom said later that night, "I've never seen anything like it. There were millionaires and paupers. Everyone, from all walks of life, loved him."

Best, children still loved this man who was 81-years-old at his death. A little girl who appeared to be around five-years-old tugged on Mary Ellen's skirt and pointed to the casket bookended at head and foot by two uniformed sheriff's deputies standing at attention. She raised her face and whispered, "That's Cawky Cawdell."

Children still swim in the Cordell Municipal Pool, named in his honor nearly thirty years after it'd been built when he was Richmond's mayor. Poorer children had had no place to swim other than streams, ponds and the dangerous Whitewater River that rushed through the city's gorge. When he was sixteen-years-old, Corky had pulled the lifeless body of a young teen from a lake's murky bottom. As mayor, it had been one of his priorities to give every child a safe, supervised place to have fun on hot summer days.

The Indiana State General Assembly passed a Senate resolution not long after his death with multiple 'whereas' paragraphs touting Corky's many accomplishments, among them sheriff, mayor, president of both the Indiana Republican Mayor and Sheriff Associations, Sagamore of the Wabash, and Boxing Hall of Fame inductee. Its concluding 'whereas' would have made him smile with modesty though he'd have been exceedingly honored and pleased.

". . . (he was) dedicated to his community and touched the lives of countless people and his death has left a void that will be impossible to fill."

Betty and Corky Cordell celebrating
their 53rd wedding anniversary
with their daughter Mary Ellen looking on
in her Avon, Indiana home in June, 1999
(He was probably saying,
"Have I told you yet today that I love you?")

44
2004-2005

Bubba, who seemed to race everywhere and get into everything like any other toddler, was seen by a cardiologist every year following his open-heart surgery when he was six months old. Each exam was followed by a good report.

Ellen's calm, quiet voice was testimony to her relief as she spoke with Debra on the telephone one hot summer night. "They said he can play any sport except football. If it weren't for that long scar – the thing runs from his little sternum straight down almost to his tummy – you'd never know he'd had that surgery. My little three-year-old buddy is such a trooper. And so is Nin! Did I tell you about her thirtieth birthday celebration?"

"No," Debra said. "But knowing you, it had to have been something else!"

"Oh, it was. We went to Disney World."

"Disneyland."

Ellen laughed. "You heard me right. Bubba's been to Disneyland. It's so close we have passes. Nin deserved a special treat, and after all, this is one of those *big* birthdays."

"Who all went? My gosh, it must've cost a fortune!"

"Well, you know everything's relative. Bob and I are still working. We are so blessed to have little Bubba, all healthy, that's the main thing. What if we hoarded money and didn't show our gratitude by having fun with our baby? It gives glory to God when we celebrate the life He's given us.

"To answer your question, though, besides Bubba, Bob and I took Nin and Traci."

Debra chuckled. "Bubba didn't have a chance! Grandpa, Grandma, his mother, aunt and Mickey Mouse to boot – all pouring attention and love on him. Poor little guy."

"Oh, he thought he was the cat's meow. Especially in his little car seat riding in the limo to LAX."

"A limo! Why am I not surprised? I've never gone anyplace with you that we haven't had the best time. You think of everything, Ellen. Everybody should be as grateful for life as you are."

"Twice as grateful!" Ellen said.

"Hey, I hafta go, but first tell me one thing that stands out about this trip."

"You're putting pressure on me. Hmmm, just one," Ellen clicked her tongue against her pallet as she mused. "Oh, I got it. Didn't happen at the theme park, but it was at one of the Disney World hotels. Bob and I had taken Bubba down to the pool and he insisted he didn't need help because he knew how to swim. He was very adamant about it so Bob let him go. Needless to say, it didn't go well and, oh I can't help but laugh: he sputtered and coughed and said to Bob, 'Maybe I don't have this swimming thing down just yet."

The girlfriends laughed their goodbyes. Hanging up the phone, Ellen continued to chuckle, remembering how Bubba had wondered where the limousine was a few days later when they'd gotten into the Suey's van for a trip to Disneyland.

45

Ellen thought she knew the importance of gratitude, of fully appreciating the gift of each day. But it wasn't until Bubba, her first grandchild, came into her life that she truly experienced the fullness of fundamental joy. Bubba made her laugh. And laugh . . .

She should write these things down. That was her thought nearly every day. The book would be too heavy to lift, she thought. Then she'd laugh again.

One of the pleasures of being grandparents was taking Bubba along with her and Bob nearly everywhere they went. Not just to Disneyland, but everyday places like their favorite diner. She and Bob didn't realize how often they sat down to eat at the D&D Cafe inside the Riverside Municipal Airport until one day four-year-old Bubba told the waitress very seriously, "I'll have the usual."

Ellen could barely catch her breath she laughed so hard. "How," she finally asked Bob, who was also attempting to regain control, "could he possibly know what that means at his age? Oh, my gosh, I'm about dying laughing!"

The tot with the thick dark hair and big brown eyes was a favorite with staff and regulars at D&D. Amid the laugher of other patrons, the waitress turned and called into the kitchen, "Bubba will have the chicken and fries!"

Bubba loved to eat his "usual" while sitting at one of the tables next to the large plate glass windows with a view of the municipal airport's tarmac. Small airplanes would land and take off just beyond the glass. But nothing thrilled the little guy like the helicopters that would hover over the building before gently drifting down to land.

"As soon as he sees a helicopter," Ellen told her mother during their next Sunday evening call, "he holds his sweet little hand up to his head as if he's shielding his eyes, except he has his hand turned backwards, and he says, 'I see a hebulor!' Bless his heart, he can't say helicopter."

Mother and daughter laughed. Marga said, "I am so anxious to see that baby. He really is getting so big. He's saying the cutest things and I want to hear them myself, just like I did that first time he came up with calling me 'mudder'."

"Oh, you will," Ellen said. "His Southwest frequent-flier card just came in the mail. He's itching to use it."

"Frequent-flier? At his age?"

"Yeah," Ellen laughed, "how many four-year-olds do you know with a frequent-flier card with Southwest? Nin jokes that Bubba has his bag packed and ready to go any time he hears Grammy and Grandpa are going someplace."

"Well, when are you coming? I haven't been treated like a queen in quite a while, you know. My baby always treats me like a queen."

"We just got back from seeing Bob's mother in Sacramento, so it may be a few weeks. We took Bubba to San Francisco, too. He loved San Francisco! He was such a good little trooper. He hiked up the hills like they were nothing. We went to Alcatraz and Angel

Island, and took the bus one day so we could show him how to navigate the big city. He was all eyes and never left my side. We've dubbed San Francisco Bubba's City."

"I can just see him. What a sweetheart. When did you say you'll be visiting?"

"Soon. But let us recover from our trip to northern California. And then Bubba has just started swimming lessons, too. Nin's baby is due in August, so it may be September before we can get to Phoenix. Can you wait that long?"

Always gracious, Ellen's mother answered, "Of course, dear. You know I'm thrilled and grateful every time you, Bob and your little man knock on my door."

"Oh, Mom! I almost forgot to tell you. You know some of the funny things Bubba says are because he's picked up on us saying them. He heard me call you Mother, so he wanted to, too . . . Mudder."

They both laughed again.

"Well, when he started swimming lessons the instructor came over and asked us what his name was after she'd talked to him. I asked what he'd told her it was. She said he told her it was 'The Man.' Bob and I laughed so hard because you know we often refer to him as The Man. I'm still laughing!"

Bubba with his grandparents and "Mudder" in Arizona

Ellen and Bob Suey with Bubba in San Francisco (2008)

46

Bubba looked past the waffles Ellen set before him. He was sitting at her large dining room table just off her Riverside kitchen. The early August morning sun streamed bright through the windows lining the countertops. Bob had his back to the open dining room, turning bacon in the Dutch oven he always used on the electric range to cook breakfast meats.

Squirming in his chair, ignoring his grammy as she poured maple syrup over melting butter on his waffle, Bubba said, "Hurry, Grandpa! I want to go meet my brother. He's waiting for me to play!"

"I'm glad you're excited to be getting a brother, Bubba," Ellen said, "but Alexander can wait until you eat your breakfast. He's probably still sleeping."

"No, he's awake. He wants to play!"

Bob turned from the stove. He and Ellen gave each other quizzical looks. Bubba was adamant. Pushing his plate away, he scooted off the chair and ran to his room. He emerged carrying two Hot Wheels cars.

At the hospital, Bob and Ellen quietly ushered Bubba into his mother's room. Nin was sitting up in bed, Chris standing beside the tiny Plexiglas bassinet between them. Inside it, wrapped like a burrito in a soft sky-blue blanket, was a miniature version of Bubba. Chris held his arms out to his first son and picked him up so he could get a good look at the baby.

Scrunching his face as if he'd just sucked a lemon, Bubba cried incredulously, "*That's* my brother?"

He wriggled from his father's arms and ran from the room. He'd seen a playroom near the nursery as he and his grandparents had walked down the hall toward his mother's room. He headed straight there. Ignoring toys and plush stuffed animals decorating the gaily painted room, he rushed to a corner and dropped to his knees as if he were hiding from the hard truth that his brother wasn't a playmate. Alexander was, of all things, a *baby*.

Chris followed his son to the playroom. "Christopher, what's the problem?"

Bubba didn't answer. He was sobbing.

Ellen came into the room in time to see Bubba turn angry eyes to his father, tears pooling and spilling onto his soft, round cheeks. She knelt beside him. "I think you had a different idea about what kind of brother you were getting. Guess we just assumed you knew he wouldn't be a big boy like you."

"Let me talk to him," Chris said.

Bubba could not be convinced nor consoled. That baby in his mother's room was not the brother he'd expected. Finally, Bob and Ellen took Bubba back to their house where they talked to him about babies and boys. Again and again.

Gradually, Bubba changed his mind about the imposter lying in the bassinet. "He can't walk or talk or anything. I'm going to have to show him how to do things. Like be a ring bearer."

He was thinking about his upcoming role at his Aunt Traci's wedding, where he would nearly steal her show with his sweet smile, mini tuxedo and irrepressible charm.

"Yes," his grammy agreed. "You are his big brother. The only one he has. And he is your only brother, too. He belongs to you."

Bubba turned large brown eyes, framed by thick, long lashes, to his grandmother. "He *is* mine! He's the best!"

Bubba as ring bearer at his Aunt Traci's wedding,
September 2005

47

2007

(The following narratives are recollections of Suzi Fryman, created from her hand-written letter to Mary Ellen Donat.)

Suzi Fryman laughed as if the joke had been on her. "I don't believe it."

Suzi was the second wife of Dave Fryman, the hunter's grandson's close friend from Dennis Junior High School. The Frymans had traveled from Boston, Indiana to Vonore, Tennessee to visit the hunter's grandson and his wife. The two couples were talking in the living room when Suzi casually mentioned that she'd been raised in Boston.

Just as casually, her husband's friend said, "My Grandpa and I found a baby in the woods outside Boston."

"Yes, we left lots of babies in the woods," Suzi laughed. "You're just teasing this old country bumpkin. You Richmond High School folks were always teasing us. I don't believe it."

The hunter's grandson left the room. He returned shortly and handed Suzi a framed newspaper article. It was the first time she'd seen the article or heard of its content.

Her laughter diminished as she read the faded newspaper account. She studied the photograph of Nurse Jenny Parrish holding the baby, then read again the story beneath it. She was intrigued.

The next week, Suzi was in the research department of Richmond's Morrisson-Reeves Library. Stephan M. Martin, Reference/Governmental Documents Librarian, helped her find then copy all the 1955 articles concerning the hunters and little Roseann Wayne.

Her next stop was the apartment of Meta Jane Benner, the widow of Boston's town marshal who'd been one of the lawmen to see the abandoned baby in the woods.

"She's beginning to have memory problems," Suzi told the hunter's grandson over the phone. "But she said, 'I remember that like it was yesterday!' Then she said 'Only about Julian telling me about the baby in the woods.' What a disappointment."

It'd been nearly ten years since Ellen Suey had written Meta, and had received the same response Mrs. Benner had just given Suzi. Ellen's conviction, that it wasn't in God's timing that she and the hunters find each other, must have been spot on. Not only did Meta not tell Suzi about her correspondence with Ellen, but Suzi was also about to run into another dead end. It involved a chance encounter with the man whose Boston front door Ellen had considered knocking on many times over the past decade.

Again, Suzi called the hunter's grandson with a research update. "I ran into John Catey at church. He said, 'I know nothing about that. I wasn't even a deputy then.' But I handed him all the newspaper clippings I had. He said he'd look into it."

John Catey was a former Wayne County sheriff who'd been one of Corky Cordell's deputies years after the abandoned-baby case. A few weeks after seeing Suzi at church, he explained to her that he didn't have the time to look into it after all.

It was, in the end, all about God's timing.

48

2013

At an after-party of a Boston High School all-class reunion, Suzi Fryman was chatting with an older alumnus when the woman suddenly brought up the long-ago tale of the baby found in the woods.

Suzi immediately asked, "You know about that?"

The woman was somewhat taken aback by her friend's peculiar enthusiasm. "Well, only that a baby was found."

Standing nearby, Dick Benner, the son of Julian and Meta, had overheard the exchange. "Yeah," he said, addressing Suzi, "my dad was town marshal then. He was there with the hunters before they took her to the hospital. That 'baby' contacted my mother several years ago. She was looking for the guys that found her . . ."

Thunderstruck, Suzi's incredulous eyes widened.

"Roseann came to town decades ago looking for the hunter," Dick Benner said. "She told my mother that she wanted to thank him for saving her life."

49

December 2013

In early December, the hunter's grandson sent a letter to John Catey. Two days later he received a reply.

Catey called him to say, "I'm going to do everything I can to get the two of you together by Christmas."

Nearly a continent away, Ellen Suey turned from the counter at McDonald's with a tray of Happy Meals for her four grandchildren and nearly bumped into a co-worker from the Department of Defense in Corona.

"Looking forward to retirement, Ellen? Bet you'll miss coming to work and having something to do every day."

Ellen shifted the fiberglass tray to balance sliding soft drinks. "Of course!" But she was reminded of the rhetorical question she'd asked her late father when he questioned her about riding in a car driven by her mother. The notion of having one free or unhappy moment in her retirement was equally amusing.

Still thinking of that day when she and her father had laughed together over her mother's marginal driving skills, she sobered. It'd been a long time since she'd had the blessing of riding in the same car with her mother. Gee whiz, it seemed like an eternity. Eight years? No, seven since Mother's passing.

Ellen's train of thought continued, but switched tracks. It was eight years since she last considered renewing the search for the hunter's grandson.

That's right, because she'd seen in the Richmond newspaper a small reference in a recurring column called "Fifty Years Ago in Richmond." It had been near the fiftieth anniversary of the day the hunter and his teenaged grandson had miraculously found her that the Richmond newspaper noted the date. And that was eight years ago.

The information for the weekly items was gathered by the husband and wife team of Jess and Lou Ann Price. "September 22, 1955," the Prices had noted, "a baby was found in the woods."

Ellen had written Jess all those years ago to ask if they'd ever found that baby. He wrote back that they hadn't. She then sent him a letter telling him simply, "I'm that baby."

He invited her to follow through on a search for the hunter, saying he'd be glad to accompany her to the *Palladium-Item* where he'd been an editor. Strong in her belief and trust in God's perfect plan, she remained true to her conviction that it wasn't yet His time, so she declined.

"Maybe I should have gone through with it," she thought briefly, smiling a farewell to her co-worker.

Ellen dismissed the idea as she set the tray of Happy Meals before four eager children, joyfully energized with Christmas excitement.

50

(The following narratives are recollections of John Catey, created from emails he sent to Mary Ellen Donat.)

John Catey was discovering that there didn't appear to be any easy way to find out who adopted Roseann, where she might be at this time, even if she was still alive.

Files were missing. Records post-1941 were still sealed. People claimed to not know anything about the nearly sixty-year-old case, didn't remember or were reluctant to reveal what they knew. And, most everyone personally involved in 1955 had passed away. The door of time was closing.

He'd paid a visit to the *Palladium-Item* newspaper offices, been helped by a reference librarian named Eric Burkhardt at Morrisson-Reeves Library, and had contacted personal friends and colleagues at the county clerk's office, vital records office and Indiana Department of Health. He talked with the current judge of Superior Court #1. All attempts led nowhere.

Even with his contacts and background – he'd been a sheriff, on Wayne County Council, on the board at the hospital, and everybody in the county either knew him personally or knew who he was – Catey's efforts were unsuccessful.

Reid Hospital told Catey they have no records of the incident, nor any records of nurses employed in 1955. He contacted a number of retired nurses he personally knew in an attempt to find Jenny Parrish. He finally was told she'd moved to Dayton, Ohio and had worked there for thirty years. She died in 2005. He tracked down her widower living in Florida, but he didn't have any recollection of the incident.

Catey even checked out a rumor that had gone around decades ago about a well-to-do family that adopted Roseann and moved to Texas. He decided he was going to start talking to anyone he could find who was alive when the baby was abandoned despite the fact that most, if not all, were now in their eighties.

www.pal-item.com Pal-1

▶ OBITUARIES

Jenny S. Britton

RICHMOND — Jenny Sue Britton, age 74, who resided in Richmond, died Monday, March 14, 2005, at Reid Hospital.

She was born Feb. 22, 1931, in Richmond to Earl and Vera Kinert Parrish and had resided in Dayton, Ohio, most of her life, moving back to Richmond 10 years ago.

She was a registered nurse and had worked at Kettering Memorial Hospital in Dayton, Ohio, for 30 years and had also been a private-duty nurse.

She was a member of First Friends Meeting, where she sang in the choir, and was a graduate of the Indiana University School of Nursing.

She is survived by two sons, Craig (Mary) Britton of Germantown, Ohio, Scott Britton of Dayton, Ohio; one grandson; a daughter-in-law, Kathy Britton of Dayton; a sister-in-law, Susie Parrish of Janesville, Wis.; and two nieces.

She was preceded in death by a brother, Ben Parrish.

A memorial service will be held Saturday at 2 p.m. in the First Friends Meeting with Doug Gwyn officiating. Burial will be in Willow Grove Cemetery.

Memorials may be made to the Help the Animals Shelter, 2101 W. Main St., Richmond, IN 47374.

Funeral arrangements are being handled by Smith & McQuiston Funeral Home in Fountain City.

031705-38472612-201

Obituary of Jenny Parrish Britton, March 2005

51

Not everyone who was somewhat connected to the case of the tiny baby left to die in remote and forbidding woods was in their eighties. Meta Jane Benner, the widow of Boston's 1955 town marshal, the man who'd been the first official to arrive at the scene, was ninety-three years old.

Meta's memory had increasingly weakened with age. When Ellen Suey wrote to her in 1998, she had been able to recall only that her husband Julian had been briefly involved in the case. When Suzi Fryman visited Meta in 2007, the widow said she remembered it like yesterday, but then didn't say anything more.

When John Catey visited Meta Jane at her apartment in The Leland, an assisted living facility in downtown Richmond, she was having a rare day of clarity.

"Oh, it's good to see you, John," she said as he bent to gently take her hand. He was still as tall and handsome as when he was a deputy sheriff alongside her husband when Corky Cordell was sheriff. "Those were good years, weren't they? Julian was so happy when Corky brought him on the department after that baby was found."

"Well, that's one of the reasons I stopped by," John said. "I was wondering if you might be able to help me find that baby, a grown woman now."

"That young lady contacted me fifteen or twenty years ago looking for the people who found her as a baby in the woods," she told John with confidence. "I can't remember her last name, but I think it began with an 'S' or a 'T'."

She was right on both counts. Ellen's married and maiden last names began with 'S' and 'T' respectively.

"I can't remember where the lady was from. It might have been Texas, Arizona or California."

She'd gotten two of the states right. Ellen's parents had retired to Arizona and she lived in California. Somehow, Meta had pulled key facts from the recesses of her diminished memory, recalling much of the content of Ellen's 1998 letter.

So now John had the first letter of a last name and possible states of residence; important clues. He'd been told that the adoptive parents may have been of significant financial means and had moved to Texas. That must mean, he reasoned, that the adoptive parents had at least a connection to Wayne County, maybe had lived there at the time of the baby's adoption.

He decided even while sitting across from Julian's frail widow that he would begin talking to anyone old enough to remember the incident.

Meta Jane Benner
(Photo provided by her son, Dick Benner)

52

After talking with Meta Benner, Catey began talking to many retired citizens, business persons, attorneys, physicians, veterinarians and others who were old enough to remember the incident. He'd talked with more than 75 people in just a couple weeks.

One of those people was a retired contractor from Cambridge City, James Sweet. He remembered a veterinarian, now deceased, who had a practice in the '40s and '50s in Mt. Auburn (a western Wayne County town not far from Cambridge City). Jim suggested to Catey that he contact veterinarian Mark Woodward, who would know more about the deceased veterinarian's family, since his parents had lived next door to them when he was growing up.

Catey decided to make the suggested call. He wanted to know what Dr. Woodward could tell him about a Mt. Auburn veterinarian by the name of Everett Test.

53

"Oh, sure," Dr. Woodward told John Catey the next day. "I remember the family well. It was Dr. Test who encouraged me to become a veterinarian."

John flipped open his notepad and clicked the end of his ballpoint pen, ready to write everything the veterinarian told him.

"They had a son named Merwin and I think his wife's name was Marga. He became a physicist. I believe he worked for the Atomic Energy Commission of the United States government at one time. They had a son and a daughter, but I don't know if they were adopted or not. The last I heard, they were living somewhere in California."

John underlined the state, one of the three recalled by Meta Jane Benner.

Back at home, he Googled the name Merwin Test. After a bit of searching, information about the late physicist appeared on John's screen. He leaned forward, his eyes rapidly scanning the lines of electronic text.

Yes, Test had lived in the Cambridge City area. His wife Marga's maiden name was Marga Mary Glunt and she was from

Union City, Indiana. She was a sister of Ruth Glunt Shendler who was married to . . .

John sat back, covered his mouth and nose with both palms, and then blew a breath that hissed quickly through his pressed hands as he stared at his computer screen in astonishment. Plain as day, there it was ". . . Marlowe M. Shendler."

Until their deaths a few years before, Ruth and Marlowe Shendler had lived less than a half mile down the road. They'd not only been neighbors for decades, but Catey's grandfather and Marlowe's mother were siblings. And those weren't their only connections.

"You won't believe what I just read," John told his wife as he walked into their family room.

Elsa Catey, still as lovely as she was the day they'd married more than fifty years before, raised her blue eyes from the package she was wrapping to put under the Christmas tree. "Getting close?"

"I don't know. But Meta Benner said Roseann's adoptive family was rumored to be of influence, that the last name might have begun with a 'T' and they might have moved to California. This man, Merwin Test, fits. But that's not the amazing thing here. The man's wife was the sister of Ruth Shendler."

"Ruth . . ." Elsa pointed in the direction of their neighbors' home. "Kevin's mom?"

John nodded. The Catey's son Mike was co-owner of Contract Industrial Tooling in Richmond. One of his employees was Kevin Shendler.

Psalm 32:8 – *The LORD says, "I will guide you along the best pathway for your life. I will advise you and watch over you."*

It's so wonderful to see how God works through ordinary people like you and me.

This shows me how with a little persistence and prayer God will reveal His plan. He gives us baby steps at first.

It was heartwarming for me to see how God weaved His plan in helping John Catey find who my adoptive parents were. I was basically right under his nose but God wasn't ready for the revealing to start.

If you have a desire, pray on it. God may say, "no," He may say, "go," or He may say, "wait." Wait on His timing; He always has the best plan.

Ellen Suey

54

December 20, 2013

It was that time of the season when very little work was getting done in offices across the country and the world. The Friday before Christmas, it seemed to Ellen Suey as if half her co-workers had taken vacation days the following Monday and the next day, too. On Tuesday, Christmas Eve, the office would clear out around noon anyway.

While friends in the office were joking and chatting, passing time until four o'clock, Ellen barely had time to eat lunch. Most of her colleagues were waiting to deal with paperwork in their in-boxes after the holiday, but Ellen was doing her best to make sure hers was empty. A date was circled on her 2014 desk calendar: Friday, January 3.

After thirty years as an administrative assistant with the Department of Defense, she would be joining her husband in retirement. She was tempted to daydream about all the home improvement projects the two planned to work on together, places they wanted to visit, or time they yearned to spend with their grandchildren. But she had too much work to clear up to think about anything beyond her computer screen. She almost hated to stop typing to answer the phone.

She was surprised to hear a familiar voice. "Ellen, it's Kevin."

What on earth? Why is he calling me at work?

The first person she called after speaking with her cousin was her husband. Bob was attending a Bible study, so was concerned when Ellen's call came. It had to be serious for her to interrupt him during class. She immediately relieved his fears by plunging right into her exciting news. "They found one of the men who found me!"

"The hunter or his grandson? You talked to him?"

"No. Kevin just called. He said his boss' dad, a former sheriff in Wayne County, has been trying to find me. The hunter is passed away, but his grandson has been trying to find me for years. Somehow, the sheriff was led to Kevin, who told him that I was the baby girl known as Roseann Wayne.

"He said the sheriff was pretty surprised."

Ellen laughed at the thought of the investigator being told by Kevin that the woman he'd been looking for was just as close as a half mile away at least once a year the past fifty-eight years. She remembered all those walks past his house. "Bob, that former sheriff is John Catey."

Bob was speechless. He knew Ellen had often been tempted to knock on Catey's door to ask for help finding the hunter and his grandson. The idea that the grandson had asked the same man to find Ellen was almost too much of a coincidence. That's when he remembered Ellen's conviction that God would, in His time, bring the two together.

"Praise God."

Ellen sighed audible relief. "Yes, praise God!"

"Now what? What's next?"

"Kevin gave me Mr. Catey's phone number. I'm supposed to call him. But, Bob, I'm just too overwhelmed to do that right now."

"By the time you get home from work it'll be late their time. Probably after eight o'clock."

"That's true. But I need some time to collect my thoughts anyway. You know how I've been wary of people who might try to say they know my birth parents or could find the men who found me. I can't shake that feeling, even though I know that Mr. Catey is sincere. And I need to compose myself to have an intelligent conversation with him.

"Let's pray about it together before I call him."

Kevin Shendler with his family;
l-r Adrienne, Vincent and Gina circa 2012

Colossians 3:14 – *Above all, clothe yourselves with love, which binds us all together in perfect harmony.*

55

December 21, 2013

7 am Pacific; 10 am Eastern

Ellen picked up her cell phone. Before tapping in John Catey's phone number, she closed her eyes then confirmed that after a night of prayer and rest, she was convinced that now was God's time. "Okay, Lord, I guess You want to open the door."

She hesitated, took a deep breath then put the phone to her ear. Feeling His assurance, she waited with pounding heart for cell towers between Riverside and Richmond to connect her to the man who had condensed fifty-eight years of separation into one extraordinary moment.

"You did this in two weeks?" Ellen asked after hearing Catey describe his exhaustive search. "That's incredible."

"I got lucky."

"You're being humble. I appreciate that. And I appreciate your persistence. For years and years I've wanted to thank the two people who found me in the woods. Whoever left me there intended for me to die. Those men saved my life. I'd like very much to speak with them."

The former sheriff told her what she already knew, that the hunter had long since passed away, but that the grandson was still living. He gave Ellen the grandson's phone number then made one request. "Will you wait a while to call him? I'd like to give him the news."

56

Despite her reservations, Ellen did call the hunter's grandson after giving John Catey time to call him first. More quickly than was comfortable for her, the man began an email and phone association. He and his wife invited Ellen and her husband to visit them in their home.

"That's just not something I'd want to do," Ellen told Bob. "I don't even know these people. It's really kind of bizarre."

Bob smiled. It was Ellen's decision and he would support her. Though she had mounting misgivings, Ellen decided to engage in a long-distance relationship.

Before she knew it, though, the hunter's grandson wanted to meet her after learning the Sueys would be in Richmond for a cousin's graduation from college.

Ellen's head was spinning at the idea. "He's moving so fast and furious, and changing his mind so much that it's making my head swim. But I can't figure out how I can say 'no' since we're already going to be in Richmond. I don't know what to do."

Bob smiled. As always, it was Ellen's decision. It wasn't long, however, before the simple meeting grew into what the hunter's grandson was calling "a reunion." He already had a guest list.

"This is going to cost us," Ellen told her husband unhappily. "We'll have to pay for a place to hold the event and a caterer, too. Well, at least half of it. And he's inviting a lot of people!"

With Bob's support, Ellen allowed plans for the reunion to continue into January even though her heart wasn't in it. She agreed with the hunter's grandson that he would find the venue and she would be responsible to find the caterer. Expenses would be shared. As it turned out, the venue was donated.

"That's a relief," Ellen sighed, giving the good news to Bob. "Now just half of the catering."

She didn't feel relief, however. The hunter's grandson was inviting more and more of his acquaintances and media to the reunion. The guest list was growing and it looked as if catering would exceed a thousand dollars.

"I don't know about this," Ellen told Debra in a phone call. "With Christmas just over and my retirement coming up . . ."

"But, isn't it cool to have a personal hero? I sure think so."

"Well, yes . . . And he's giving glory to God. That's what's really important, because there's really only one Hero."

57

January 2014

“This is cool,” Ellen was thinking as she pulled her van, fondly nicknamed Ethel, to a stop behind a maroon Ford. She was in the pick-up line at Riverside Christian School. Recently retired, she smiled to herself.

“This really is so cool. I never got to do this with my kids. And now here I am, picking up Bubba from school. Where next? Dairy Queen? Oh, yeahhh.”

The school’s double doors opened. An orderly line of uniformed students emerged. Little ones. Kindergartners first, Ellen mused. “Oh, how quick they grow!”

It was just a couple years ago, when Bubba was ten years old, Ellen remembered as she watched more students march into the California sunshine, that he told me he was getting too old to be called Bubba. Ellen smiled at the memory. “I will call you Bubba at your high school graduation,” she’d said.

Her grin drifted into a melancholy smile as she relived that moment. He’d hugged her and said, “Okay, Grammy.”

Aloud, she said to herself with a sigh, “Oh, what a sweet smile.”

And there it was again as he stepped into the sunlight from the school and spied Ethel in the line of cars.

Ellen stepped from the van as Bubba approached. He put his arm proudly around her shoulder. Excited to be nearly as tall as she, he smirked, "Hi, Grammy."

Though he was enjoying this moment in front of his classmates, Bubba dropped his arm. Tossing his backpack into Ethel's backseat, he hopped in the front beside his grammy. It was a half-day for middle school. Alexander and their sister Alexa were in elementary school. This would be a special afternoon with only Grammy.

"Where do you want to go for lunch?" she asked, excited to have alone-time with her first-heart.

It was the same scene and the same question all that week. Five precious days, just the two of them. Bubba picked a different restaurant each day. And, of course, one of them was D&D Café where he could watch small planes and "hebulors" take off and land.

Ellen's grandchildren Alexa, Alexander,
and Bubba holding Aiden (December 2013)

58

Two weeks later, Grammy and Bubba once again had alone-time. But not so special since Bubba wasn't feeling well. It seemed that he'd eaten an entire bag of gummy bears.

"The whole half-pound?" Ellen asked her daughter-in-law.

"I guess we shouldn't be surprised," Nin answered. "He's a typical twelve-year-old. But it sure did make him sick. Can you watch him for me today?"

"That's why I retired. To spend more time with my grandchildren. Bring him over."

Ellen expected Bubba to feel better by noon, after he'd digested the gooey candy. Instead, he slept and stayed stretched out on the living room couch for most of the day. And the next one, too. By Wednesday, though, he was full of energy. Ellen knew she couldn't keep him lying or even sitting on the couch if she'd tried.

The only thing to do, she told him with a twinkle in her eye and voice, was to take him to lunch. He wolfed down his cheeseburger, taking huge bites as if he were already a teenager. With mouth full, he talked excitedly about soccer try-outs the next day at Riverside Christian School.

The next afternoon Ellen was walking her dogs Sarah and Opie when she received a phone call from the secretary at her grandchildren's school. The woman wanted to know if Ellen could pick up Alexander and Alexis, then keep them at her house. Ellen heard the calm voice on the other end explain, "Bubba collapsed while running during soccer try-outs. He's at the hospital."

Ellen called Bob at work to ask that he leave to be with Chris, Nin and Bubba while she kept the younger two at their house. A couple hours later Bob called from Parkview Hospital.

Bubba had passed away.

His grammy numbly continued to hold the phone to her ear as she stared at the front door. Her mind reeled to the previous afternoon when Nin had come after work to pick up her exuberant son. Bubba had stepped through the threshold then turned back to grin at his grandmother. He'd waved in that hurried way young boys do, then trotted to his mother's car.

Stunned, Ellen continued to hold the phone to her ear. She stared at her tightly closed front door and relived that happy moment. Bubba, just on the other side of the threshold, turning to smile at her as he waved goodbye.

She lowered the phone limply to her side and said aloud as if in a fog, "Little did I know that would be the last time I will ever see my sweet boy here on earth."

Psalm 34:18 – *The LORD is close to the brokenhearted and saves those who are crushed in spirit.*

This day was a sad day for our family. The Lord called our sweet Bubba home and I didn't understand why.

I know that Bubba had accepted Jesus as his Lord and Savior. What I didn't realize was the 23rd Psalm was Bubba's favorite scripture.

When something like this happens and especially with a child it makes you realize how fragile and short life is. Handle it with prayer and love.

This is something that we will never get over; just through. It gives me a better understanding and empathy for others who have lost a loved one so young.

Ellen Suey

59

March 2, 2014

Shortly following her husband's 2003 death, Betty Cordell had moved into the Leland Residence, which were senior apartments before it became an assisted living facility. While packing for the move, Mary Ellen came across her mother's worn address book. Its pages were falling out, additions were made in margins, and deceased friends' names were crossed off. Obviously, her mother needed another address book. Mary Ellen began to transfer names from old to new. If she or Betty didn't recognize an entry, it wasn't transferred.

Beside Ellen Suey's name, address and phone number in the old book there was no parenthetical notation that she was known to them as Rose Wayne. That's how she was lost to Corky's wife and daughter. Until a snowy March Sunday a decade later.

It was nearly noon, but Tom and Mary Ellen Donat had just finished a breakfast of potato pancakes and link sausage after attending early church service. The table cleared, Mary Ellen opened her laptop. Check e-mail, see what's happening on Facebook, go to the *Palladium-Item*'s site to read Richmond obituaries.

That was her regular computer routine.

Rarely did she read the *Palladium*'s online articles. She and Tom had been gone from Richmond nearly fifteen years now, and since her mother's passing in 2012, Mary Ellen didn't keep up with the Rose City's news. As soon as her hometown newspaper's home page appeared, it was her habit to immediately click on "Obituaries." Sometimes, if an article was written by her friends and former colleagues Bill Engle or Rachel Sheeley, she would read it. Today though, she was ready for a nap. But first, she wanted to see if there was someone she knew who needed a sympathy card.

She clicked on the *P-I online* menu bar and a funeral notice appeared. But in that brief moment between front page and obituaries, her eye had caught a vintage photograph of a nurse holding a baby. She couldn't possibly have read the caption above the grainy photo, yet she clearly saw the words in her head. "Tiny Baby Girl Found In Woods At Boston."

She quickly clicked back to the News page.

The article was written by Bill Engle. The headline shouted 'IF HE HADN'T FOUND ME, I WOULD HAVE DIED.' There was also an obviously dated photo of a teenager with an older man. A subhead beneath the two photographs read, "Decades-long search reunites ex-Richmond man with baby he rescued from certain death."

"Dad!" Mary Ellen said aloud as if he were standing right there. "It's Rose Wayne!"

Corky and the grown baby had kept in contact on and off for several years following Ellen's 1982 visit. Correspondence slowed and then stopped as in his later years Corky's health had increasingly failed. Like her father, Mary Ellen once in a while wondered about the baby found in the woods. She'd regretted losing touch with the woman. She would have liked to have let her know about her dad's death. It was an irony that it had been she herself who'd dismissed Ellen Suey's contact information from her mother's tattered address book.

The article was long and included several photos. A coveted Sunday feature story. Engle had written an excellent narrative with lots of detail and quotes. There was a large color photograph of Ellen Suey with her husband, children and four grandchildren.

"Look at this, Tom," Mary Ellen called. "It's Rose Wayne. Isn't she pretty? She looks so young! And Bill wrote the story. He talked to her!"

Her husband came from the family room to look over her shoulder. He, too, had heard many times from his father-in-law the story of the baby found by the hunter in the woods. "There's a picture of John Catey, too. What'd he do?"

"The cutline says he found the grown Roseann . . . that's what the story says, that she was called Roseann. I never heard that before. Dad always called her Rose Wayne."

She thought of how happy her father would be. "I heard about her all my life. It's like a Disney princess just jumped right out of my computer. I wonder . . ."

Mary Ellen clicked on the menu bar at the top of her screen to return to Facebook. She typed "Ellen Suey" in the social network's search bar. Up popped "Ellen Suey, Riverside, CA." That's what Bill had written: She lives in Riverside. Mary Ellen clicked on the link and there was Ellen smiling at her from the same photograph she'd supplied the *Palladium* for the Sunday feature.

Heart racing, Mary Ellen private-messaged the iconic heroine of her childhood. "Good morning, Ellen. I'm Corky Cordell's daughter. He spoke of you often, always with thankfulness and awe. He was so proud of you, and loved it when you visited or wrote. I hope you'll accept my FB-friend request; it would please him so much. Blessings to you!"

Almost immediately she heard a bubble tone. Ellen had accepted her friend request.

There would be no napping today. She was far too thrilled for that. It was as if in a supernatural, emotional way she'd also connected with her father. No, it was much more than a metaphor; ten years after his death, her father's presence was palpable.

She could literally feel his joy.

60

BILL ENGLE'S ARTICLE

(Reprinted with Bill Engle's permission)

Palladium Item (front page with color photographs)
March 2, 2014

"If He Hadn't Found Me, I would Have Died"
Decades-long search reunites ex-Richmond man with baby he rescued from certain death

By Bill Engle Staff Writer

Dave Hickman remembers it like it was yesterday, the day 58 years ago that changed his life forever.

The 73-year-old Tennessee man was then a 14-year-old Richmond kid, hunting with his grandfather, Clay Smith, in woods just west of Boston Ind.

He and his grandfather, a man he idolized for the doting care he brought to their relationship, had just finished hunting and had begun skinning squirrels in a field off Indiana 122.

It was shortly after 6 p.m. Sept. 22, 1955.

A noise interrupted their post-hunt reverie, like a soft cry or coo. They heard it again.

Hickman decided to find out what it was, a harmless, curious decision that saved a human life.

He walked the fence row for about 25 yards where the noise seemed to emanate. Then he started to climb the fence.

"When I was on top of the fence I saw her," Hickman said.

It was a tiny baby, alone, chilled, drenched from the overnight rain, wrapped in a towel, umbilical cord coagulated to the fabric of the towel.

Police later said she was there for 12 to 24 hours. Doctors said she was no more than 5 to 6 days old.

There was no doubt she had been left there to die.

"Every day I see that vision of her laying in the brush and sticks and she was looking up at me. She wasn't crying. It was more like she was cooing. You could tell she had been there a while," Hickman said.

"It was a shock. You just would never think you would find a baby laying out there. I remember thinking, "What kind of a person would do something like this?"

The two rescued the infant, called the Wayne County Sheriff Department and the baby was whisked away to Reid Hospital where she was treated.

She was named Roseann Wayne, Roseann because the people in the Wayne County Welfare Department, in whose custody she was placed, liked the name and Wayne for Wayne County.

Authorities never determined who dumped the baby along the roadside. A faint laundry mark on the towel in which she was wrapped was their only clue.

The welfare department fielded a dozen calls from couples wanting to adopt the baby. Applicants were recorded and told no plans for the baby's future would be made until she was strong enough to leave the hospital.

The child survived and began to grow.

Hickman, a man of strong Christian faith has been haunted by the memory throughout his life, including his recollection of the day months later at Dennis Middle School when he was called to the office to find two nurses and Baby Roseann.

"She was being adopted out and they brought her so I could hold her, to say goodbye," Hickman said. "She was so beautiful, sound asleep, wrapped in a blanket. My emotions just took over."

Hickman's Search

Flash forward 58 years to Dec, 9, 2013. John Catey of Richmond opened a letter from Hickman asking for Catey's help in finding Baby Roseann. Hickman said he and his wife Gaile had been searching for 40 years for the infant he found in the woods.

"He said he continually wondered what happened to Roseann and how wonderful it would be to just talk to her and find out what her life has been like," Catey said.

Over the years, Hickman had written officials at Wayne County, Reid Hospital, and Palladium Item seeking information. He even wrote to former sheriff Edward "Corky" Cordell. He got nowhere.

Finally, he wrote to Catey, the retired two-term Wayne County sheriff and former county commissioner and councilman. Catey was up to the task.

He immediately called Hickman, who lives in Vonore, Tenn., a town of 1,462 south and west of Knoxville.

"He told me, 'I'm going to do everything I can to get you two together by Christmas,'" Hickman said. "I thought that would be a miracle."

Catey found court information on adoptions and welfare records concerning juveniles remain sealed and not open to the public, so he resorted to old-fashioned dogged police work to find clues. He used his contacts in the county and in county government, his knowledge of the area and his own determination.

Still, he moved systematically from one clue to the next.

"I'll bet I talked to 75 people, bankers, attorneys, nurses, physicians, veterinarians. I knew they had to be old to remember this. They've got to be 80 or better," Catey said.

"I got lucky."

At 9 a.m. on Dec 22, Catey called Hickman at home in Tennessee.

"He said, 'Write down this name and write down this phone number.' He said, 'Dave, that's your Roseann.' I had been trying to find her. I had spent so many years worrying about what had happened to her.

"It was truly amazing," he said.

Hickman called.

"When I heard her voice, I couldn't talk. The emotions overcame me," Hickman said. "I gave the phone to my wife, and she talked to her. After a little bit, then I could talk to her. There was an instant bond between Ellen and me.

"It's almost as if she was my baby. It certainly has had quite an effect on me," he said.

Catey's Search

In fewer than 30 days, Catey had found Mary Ellen Suey. For Catey, it was like a police investigation.

"That's my background," he said. "You just keep digging until you find something to build on."

For instance, Catey wanted to talk with Julian Benner, former Boston town marshal, who helped with the rescue and the investigation into the baby's abandonment, but Benner was deceased.

So he talked to Benner's widow, Meta Jane, who remembered the last name of the family who adopted Roseann "might" have started with the letter "T". Meta Jane also told Catey a woman had come around in the early 1990s, looking for the two who had found the baby.

Another source said the family who adopted the baby was a prominent one in Wayne County.

Retired Cambridge City contractor Jim Sweet gave Catey the name Dr. Everett Test, a veterinarian who lived in the area in the 1950s before moving to Maryland. Sweet told him to talk to veterinarian Dr. Mark Woodward, who knew Everett Test.

Woodward gave Catey the name of Test's son and his wife, Merwin and Marga Test.

Catey used that information to establish a family relationship that landed him on the doorstep of Kevin Shendler, who lives south of Richmond. Shendler works for Catey's son Mike at Contract Industrial Tooling in Richmond, and the Shendlers live down the road from Cateys.

"(Shendler) said that Merwin and Marga Test had adopted a baby girl known as Roseann Wayne and her name was now Mary Ellen Suey and she was living in Riverside Calif," Catey said. "I was pretty surprised."

He asked Shendler to contact Suey to find out if it was all right for him to call her. Catey then called to confirm she was the baby Roseann Wayne and to ask if it was OK to give her number to Dave Hickman.

"She told me she had been looking for him for years and that she very much wanted to talk to him," Catey said.

"It was exciting to hear from John Catey," Ellen Suey said recently from her home in Riverside, Calif. "It was like getting back a piece of my own personal history that I never thought I'd get back."

"John Catey's the real hero here," Hickman said. "I can't thank him enough."

Since that day

Suey's family had moved to Silver Springs, Md., and in 1964, they moved to California.

She worked for 30 years as an executive assistant for the U.S. Defense Department in California, but she has come back to the Richmond area every year to visit her aunt Ruth Shendler.

Suey married, had two children, divorced and has been married to her second husband, Bob Suey for 19 years. They had four grandchildren, though one died tragically in January.

"She's a very lovely lady, a strong Christian," Hickman said.

Hickman graduated Richmond High School in 1960, served for three years in the U.S. Army, moved to Florida with his family and worked his whole life in construction. He retired in Florida before moving to Tennessee eight years ago.

He returns to Richmond regularly for reunions with five close friends.

Hickman and Suey have become close friends and stay in contact almost daily. When Suey's grandson died, the Hickmans called and sent cards and flowers.

They plan to meet in Richmond in May.

"He's my hero," Suey said of Hickman. I'm pretty sure that whoever placed me (in the field near Boston) placed me there to die. If he hadn't found me, I would have died."

But Hickman refuses to be called a hero.

"I'm just very fortunate I was there," he said. "I found her because God allowed me to save her life. I'm so pleased that He honored me to find her."

"He said the Lord's my hero and I said, 'I understand that, but you're my hero here on earth.'" Suey said.

Both said the reunion will be very emotional.

"But they are going to be happy tears," Suey said. "He will see that I lived a good life. They are good people, and now we consider Dave and Gaile part of our family."

"I'm really looking forward to that so much," Hickman said. "It's a wonderful end to the story, but it won't be an end. It's just a beginning."

Suey continues to work to unseal her adoption case file and find out what she can about her birth parents.

"I'm very inquisitive. I want to know why things happened this way, the where," she said

She has asked Hickman to take her to the spot where he found her.

"I always wonder, why did they pick this spot? I guess I can look at the spot as that's where I started my life, right there. That's where I get my life back," she said.

61

Spring 2014

"This dog is going to a schnauzer rescue. He's a mess."

Mary Ellen Donat wasn't happy that the pitiful, abused Heinz 57 they'd adopted from Richmond's HELP the Animals shelter three weeks before was still terrorizing their fourteen-year-old cat.

"We can't," Tom said, hugging the emaciated yearling who was just learning to eat from a dish and had finally gotten used to a collar and leash.

That afternoon, Tammy Shendler came to both Tom's and Tooey's rescue. "I know a trainer in your area who can help you."

After Ellen Suey had accepted her Facebook friend request, Mary Ellen had received one from Tammy. She hadn't recognized the name, but if she was a friend of Ellen's, she came with good credentials. It wasn't long, though, before she and Tammy were having phone conversations as if they'd known each other for decades. In fact, as it turned out, they had. Tammy's son and Mary Ellen's daughter were classmates in the same preschool class in the mid-eighties.

Early in their renewed friendship, Mary Ellen was unaware of Tammy's role in helping Ellen discover the unspeakable circumstances of her first days of life. All she knew was that Tammy and Ellen were related by marriage. Her friendships with the cousins-in-law were taking a slow, natural course; the kind that would endure.

In his March article, Bill Engle had quoted the hunter's grandson describing his relationship with the woman who'd been left as an infant to die in the woods. "There was an instant bond between Ellen and me."

It would have seemed that way. In the haze of her grief and the swiftness with which the hunter's grandson moved along with the reunion and continued to promote the event in various media, Ellen was, in reality, merely going through motions.

"Everything," she told Mary Ellen less than a year later near her Riverside home, "was moving too fast. And everyone seemed to think it was such a fairy tale. I didn't want to disappoint anyone."

Touching the scars that discolor and mar her jawline, she told Mary Ellen that sunny February 2015 day as they walked in the lapping surf of Newport Beach, "But it's not a fairy tale. It's a story about God's grace and His divine intervention. All glory belongs to Him."

Back in the spring of 2014, Mary Ellen was just touching the surface of what was to be a blessed and profound friendship. She loved learning through Facebook postings about Ellen's current life and her strong commitment to Christ. Tammy, too, was a believer.

The sheriff's daughter could hardly wait to meet the two women. Ellen had invited the Donats to the May rendezvous in Richmond that was being referred to as a reunion. It was intended to be a celebration. Invitations to the event included Tammy Shendler, Suzi Fryman, Bill Engle and his wife Jeanne . . . and Mary Ellen would represent her father, Corky Cordell. Just as she'd been unaware of Tammy's role in helping Ellen to discover she'd been left to die as an infant, Mary Ellen had no idea as she prepared to attend the reunion that Ellen was growing increasingly uneasy about the event.

The week following the publication of Bill's March article, the hunter's grandson and Ellen fielded dozens of calls from television networks, magazines and internet media groups. *USA Today* designated Bill Engle's account the #1 Inspirational Story of the Week.

"Obviously, I was there," she told Debra after one journalist's call, "but of course I don't remember a thing. It's sort of comforting to have an idea of what happened, so I want to believe what he's saying about that day. That's why I've been agreeing with things he's been saying. I just feel uneasy about it because there aren't any other people still alive who were there. Except little old me."

A producer from CBS Morning News, who'd picked up Bill's story from a wire service, called. The daily news program wanted to know if it could cover the reunion. It was decided that the first meeting of the baby and one of the men who'd found her would make a topical story. CBS Morning News would send a New York producer and camera crews from their Dayton, Ohio and Indianapolis station affiliates.

The tiny baby found in the woods would once again make national news.

62

May 4, 2014

Richmond, Indiana's Historic Depot District

The rich dark wood of Maria Mitrione's Italian Market's Rosemary Room in Richmond's historic Depot District was offset by glass windows on two sides that let in bright light from the deli. A caterer had set up his tables in the brick building just outside the double-door entrance to the Rosemary Room on the ground floor. Inside, more than fifty people waited for the hunter's grandson to arrive. He was to make an entrance.

Ellen had been instructed to arrive earlier and wait for him with other guests. She'd brought scrapbooks and photographs that portrayed the stages and events of her life. They were propped on tables along the back wall. Guests milled around the display, but mingled with each other, too. The room was abuzz with chatter, laughter and anticipation.

Oddly, the subject of all the attention was receiving very little. She was quietly standing with Bob in the Rosemary Room, so inconspicuous that Mary Ellen was surprised when Tammy pointed her out.

"That's her? Gosh, nobody would guess. Why isn't she being introduced with fanfare along with the hunter?"

Tammy shrugged, lifting her eyebrows to silently communicate the obvious: "Good question."

When the grown teenager walked into the Rosemary Room, the waiting crowd stood and cheered, vigorously applauding. As designed, he stopped in the doorway to accept the accolades. Among familiar faces of those looking on were Mayor Sally Hutton, John and Elsa Catey, Kevin and Gina Shendler, the perplexed Donats . . . and Ellen.

Even if she hadn't been a striking woman, with full, long, dark hair and blue eyes that shone from fashionable eyeglasses, it would have been surprising that she had been relegated to the role of supporting cast. She played her part well, sitting demurely in a straight-back chair until she received a cue to stand and greet the hunter's grandson. After embracing, both crying and laughing at once, the two leaned apart to look at one another.

"This is the part," Ellen prompted, "where you say 'You look so different!'"

Nearly every man and woman in the room had tears in their eyes, many overflowing. Ellen's children, their spouses and Ellen's grandchildren, who were Skyping from California, also wiped away tears.

A few nights later, as the Sueys lay awake in the guest room of her cousin Kevin Shendler's home, Ellen and Bob whispered regrets about the disappointing reunion.

Bob soothed his wife's qualms as she recounted the day and subsequent news reports. "Remember what's important. We have two wonderful kids, three beautiful grandchildren and one grandchild who's waiting for us in Heaven."

Ellen nodded in the dark, remembering something Bubba had said shortly before his unexpected death in January.

"If God hadn't used those hunters to find you, none of us would be here."

Mary Ellen Donat with Ellen Suey at their first meeting; the Reunion, May 4, 2014

63

BILL ENGLE'S REUNION ARTICLE

(Reprinted with Bill Engle's permission)

Palladium Item
May 5, 2014

Rescuer, Woman reunited

Hunter, Baby he found in the woods reconnect after 58 years

It was a reunion 58 years in the making,

Dave Hickman, who as a 14-year-old boy found an infant girl in a woods south of Richmond, was reunited with her Sunday afternoon in an emotional gathering at Maria Mitrione's Italian Market in the city's Depot District.

About 50 family, friends and well-wishers watched as Hickman, now living in Vonore, Tenn., walked into Mitrione's Rosemary Room and into the arms of Ellen Suey, the woman whose life Hickman saved Sept. 22, 1955.

"I've been waiting for this for 58 years," Hickman said as he looked into her eyes, rubbed her shoulders and fought back tears.

"You're my hero," said Suey, who now lives in Riverside, Calif. "This is amazing."

Hickman clearly at a loss for words before Suey smiled and said, "This is the part where you say, 'You look so different.'"

Hickman was hunting with his grandfather, Clay Smith, in a woods along Indiana 122, west of Boston, when he investigated an odd cooing sound. He walked 100 yards and suddenly saw a baby laying in a pile of brush. He and his grandfather called the sheriff and the baby was taken to Reid Hospital.

The child was named Roseann Wayne and was adopted by a couple who soon left the area.

Hickman had been searching for her for years. In December 2013, he contacted former Wayne County commissioner, councilman and sheriff John Catey.

Catey turned the search into a personal mission, interviewing more than 75 people and looking up records at the Wayne County Courthouse, Morrisson-Reeves Library and online before finding Ellen Suey in California.

"It was just fun to see if I could piece this all together and put them together," Catey said at the reunion Sunday. "I'm just really thrilled for the two of them and appreciative that I could play a role in that."

"I think Ellen was resigned to the fact that she would never find the men who found her," said Suey's husband Bob. "John played a significant role. It's an amazing story already and it's great to now bring it to a conclusion."

"If it hadn't been for John, I don't know if this would have happened," Ellen Suey said.

Hickman brought the room to tears when he presented Ellen Suey three roses, noting, "that this is our third reunion."

"The first rose is for a little baby girl that God led my grandfather and me to find in the woods. The second is for the little baby girl named Roseann Wayne that two angels brought to me to say good-bye when I was in school," he said.

"The third rose is for today and for a very special lady who was saved by the hand of God, Mary Ellen Suey," Hickman said.

"Right now I'm just kind of numb," Ellen Suey said. "I'm just so excited to finally meet him. It's just so nice to meet him and give him a hug and thank him for what he did. If it wasn't for him I wouldn't be here."

"She will always be my little girl," Hickman said.

Elaine Buckler came to the reunion Sunday to meet both Hickman and Ellen Suey. Buckler's family lived across the road from the woods where Hickman found the baby.

"(Hickman) and his grandfather came to our house to call the sheriff and then my father (Paul) went with them to wait for the deputies," Buckler said. "It's really exciting to be here. I get chills thinking about it.

"This is a story that has always been a topic of conversation in our family," Buckler said.

Ken Jordan and Matt Mercurio also attended the reunion. They were part of the Richmond High School graduating class with Dave Hickman and have remained close.

"It was a really close class," Mercurio said. "We ran around together and have stayed close friends."

"It's good to be here. We grew up on the west side together. This is a very special day for Dave," Jordan said.

Richmond Mayor Sally Hutton also attended the reunion.

"This story just says that you never give up. You follow your hopes and dreams and believe that it can be done," she said. "It also shows that we have a lot of good people here, always have and always will."

64

May 5, 2014

Despite being tied onto the wire fence two days earlier, the three pink ribbons fluttered in the fog as fresh as if they'd been placed there just that morning. A line of cars were pulled onto the same patch of gravel that had been the parking spot of two hunters 58 years before.

Drivers and passengers emerged from their vehicles solemn as mourners. They walked along the road's berm about fifty yards and stopped where the three pink ribbons marked the place Ellen had lain as an infant wounded, soaking wet and near death.

Wearing a blue jean jacket against the Indiana chill, Ellen stood in front of the three pink ribbons the hunter's grandson had tied on the wire fence. She hadn't seen him since they'd left the Italian Market the afternoon before.

"Did you put these ribbons here?" she asked him.

"Yes," he said simply.

For long solemn moments, everyone was quiet. Family, friends, and media remained respectfully near the road, unobtrusive. Ellen stared into the woods, then slowly turned her head to take in the vast, desolate landscape around them. For as far as she could see, there was not a sign of civilization. The two-lane road stretched from rising to setting sun, separating only acres and acres of field from the equally vast stand of woods behind her.

"Now it's clear to me," she said. "I was left here to die."

65

BILL ENGLE'S ARTICLE ABOUT THE SITE

(Reprinted with Bill Engle's permission)

Palladium Item
May 6, 2014

'I was left here to die'

Ellen Suey glanced over the fence and then looked around at rolling Indiana farmland.

"Now it's clear to me. I was left here to die," she said.

"No question about it," said Dave Hickman.

Hickman on Monday took Suey to the exact spot in Wayne County - five miles south of Richmond and a half mile east of U.S. 27 on Indiana 122-where he found Suey on Sept. 22, 1955. Experts estimated Suey was five to six days old and had lain in a brush pile along a fence line 12 to 24 hours.

She was wrapped in a towel and her umbilical cord was coagulated to her body.

She was abandoned but cooing just loud enough to catch Hickman's attention. Hickman, who was 14 at the time, had just finished hunting with his grandfather, Clay Smith.

On Monday, Hickman, who is retired and lives in Vonore, Tenn., told Suey the story of that day.

"It was a typical Indiana day, cold in the morning but it warmed up later in the afternoon," he said. "We had just got done squirrel hunting, and I kept hearing this sound. It wasn't a baby's cry. It was more like a low cooing.

"I walked about 50 yards along the fence line and just stopped in this spot. The weeds were grown up so I started climbing over the fence. When I got to the top of the fence and was about to step down, that's when I saw you. You were just laying there in a brush pile looking up at me.

"It's a sight I've seen in my mind for the last 58 years," he said.

Emotion got the best of Hickman as he told his story Monday.

"It's the same emotion I felt when I found you that day," he told Suey.

Suey, who now lives in Riverside, Calif., stood and took in the countryside -deserted, a slight dip in the road, not a farmhouse in sight.

"I guess I feel kind of numb," she said. "I can't get my head around how somebody could do that. You don't just dump a baby in the woods. They meant to kill me. If it wasn't for Dave . . .

"Right now, I just want answers," Suey said. "Why? Why did you do this to me?"

"I want whoever did this to meet my mother and father, especially my mother, and thank them for raising me," Suey said.

"Carrying a baby for nine months and then just taking it and dumping it. I can't understand that, either," Hickman said.

Hickman brought his two sons to the spot on Saturday "So they could see the exact spot that has had such an effect on my whole life."

He tied three pink ribbons to the fence to symbolize the three times he had met Suey; when he found her, when two nurses brought her to his school when she was adopted three months later and Sunday when they had a grand reunion at Maria Mitrione's in the Richmond Historic Depot District.

"This spot will always be sentimental to me," he said. "And I will always think of you as my little girl."

"This is my woods." Suey said. "And the Good Lord directed you to me."

They held hands, then paused, and hugged as both realized how much their lives had changed on that very spot 58 years ago.

66

Anyone who'd read Bill Engle's story and then tried to find the site would have had a hard time. The landscape and fence row was nondescript. Even with road coordinates, it would be nearly impossible to find the exact spot because there were no ribbons on the fence. Someone had removed them sometime between the Monday gathering at the site and the following morning.

When Ellen heard about the missing ribbons she had one thought: it must have been someone who knew precisely where she'd been left to die. Someone who didn't want bright evidence of that coldblooded act to wave on that fence like a commemorative flag.

Ellen recalled what Corky Cordell had told her thirty-two years before. "If the people who left you there ever came forward, or were discovered, they'd have to stand trial for what they've done. It was attempted murder, abandoning a helpless baby in the woods."

She called Debra, who responded with shock. "I don't know how anyone can live with themselves all these decades knowing they dumped a little baby girl in the woods and left her to die.

There are so many unanswered questions. In my opinion this case is still unresolved and I feel in order for justice to be served, and for your peace of mind, it should be resolved."

"I don't hold any animosity towards my birth parents," Ellen said. "I would feel better if I knew they and the person who abandoned me know the Lord and have asked for forgiveness. Whoever left me in the woods to die is going to have to answer to God one day for what they did.

"I am so very blessed to have been adopted into a Christian home with wonderful parents. Just shows how God works and His plans are better than ours could ever be. I claim Matthew 18:5 for my mom and dad: 'Whoever receives one child in My name receives Me.'"

Jeremiah 29:11 also came to Ellen's mind. "For I know the plans I have for you, declares the Lord, plans to prosper you and not to harm you, plans to give you hope and a future."

The lonely stretch of road near Boston, Indiana
(photo taken May 5, 2014).

67

Not long after Bill's first article appeared in the Palladium-Item, Ellen received a letter from a Richmond attorney (referred to in this memoir as L.A.). In it, L.A. advised Ellen that a personal friend and client (identified in this memoir as M.W.) thought she might be the sister of her biological mother. Usually wary of such claims, Ellen decided to give him a call.

She asked if the woman might be her biological mother. L.A. flatly said she was not. He told Ellen that M.W. thought only that her sister, a childhood friend of L.A.'s who had passed away decades before, may be her mother.

It appeared to Ellen that he was keeping something from her; it was a strong intuition. She told him what Corky had said about prosecution.

L.A. said with curt authority, "Oh, no, that doesn't apply."

(Ellen told Mary Ellen in a text message later that spring as they were discussing L.A.'s strange, secretive behavior concerning anything to do with Ellen's case, "I found that odd since my attorney had told me your father was right." L.A. had also inexplicably and suddenly stated to Ellen during a visit to his office, "I was (in college) at the time and nowhere near Richmond.")

During the March phone call, L.A. requested that Ellen send photographs so M.W. could determine if there was a family resemblance. Ellen said she would, but there was something else on her mind.

In late December, following Catey's call, Ellen had begun to look for her biological parents. Like her mother, Marga, she'd forgiven them. She just wanted to know who they were, to have access to health information for herself and her children, especially after Bubba's sudden collapse and death on the soccer field.

Although Ellen didn't know L.A., she asked if he could help have her adoption records opened. She mentioned to him that the late attorney John Harlan, a close college friend of her adoptive father's, had handled their case and she planned to ask his partners to show her his records.

L.A. told her he'd get the Harlan records. They were, however, never produced. (Months later, Mary Ellen Cordell Donat asked a longtime friend who was one of Harlan's partners if she could get copies for Ellen. Harlan's partner looked for the legal papers, but told her he was unable to locate any files at all for Merwin, Marga or Mary Ellen Test.)

Not long after sending the photographs to L.A., Ellen received a call from him requesting that she submit to a DNA test. She agreed to the test, and it was performed under L.A.'s supervision in early May 2014 during Ellen's visit to Indiana.

On May 16th Ellen received a letter from L.A. He'd also sent copies to the testing doctor, to John Catey, and three women who had contacted him saying they believed M.W.'s sister was Ellen's biological mother. The letter informed them that the DNA test had returned negative.

L.A. seemed to be covering all the bases even though only Ellen and M.W. were principally involved. M.W. had paid for both the DNA test and L.A.'s time, but had not given permission for results of the test to be divulged to third parties. Ellen was baffled by L.A.'s insistence to not only her and M.W., but also to a number of others that there was no relationship between the baby abandoned in the woods and his childhood friend.

Despite L.A.'s assertion, physical and medical similarities convinced Ellen and M.W. that they were indeed related. So, the two had a second DNA test performed without L.A.'s involvement or knowledge. It returned 58.3 percent positive for an aunt to niece relationship. That number confirmed the two women's suspicions.

The second DNA test results revealed that it was highly likely that Ellen had indeed discovered the identity of her birth mother.

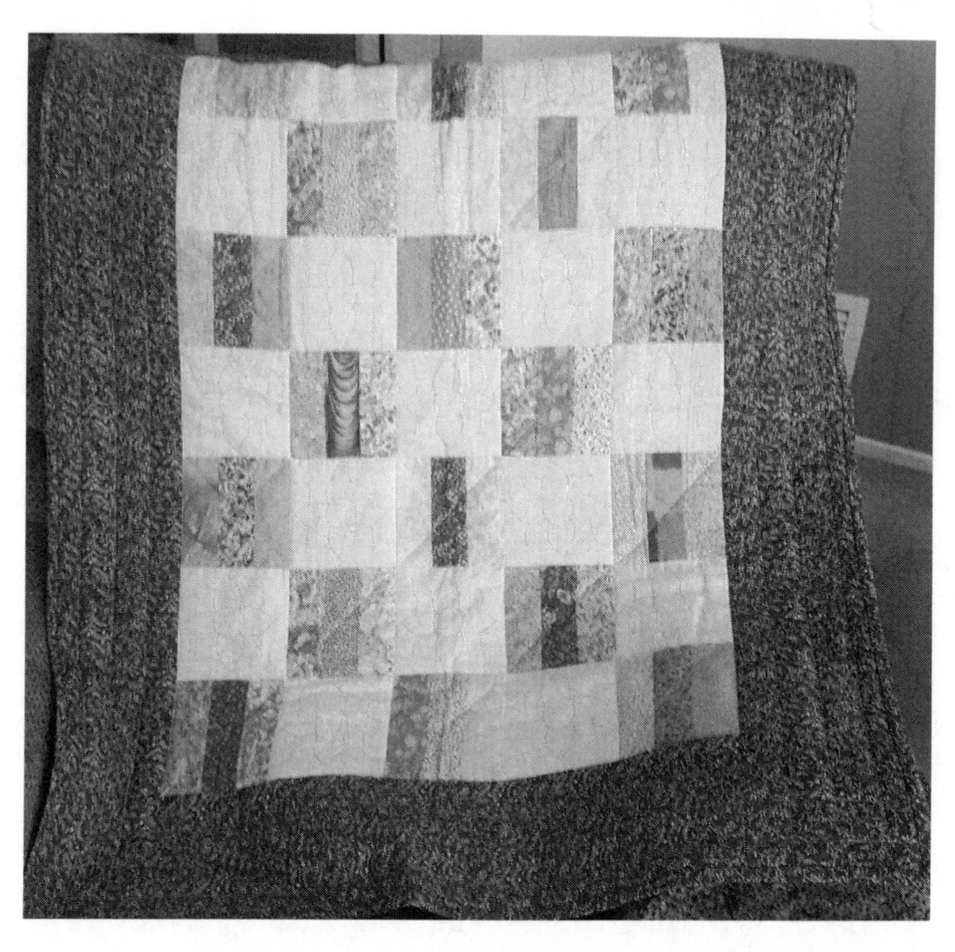

A baby blanket made by M.W.
and presented to Ellen with the sentiment,
"You should have had it a long time ago."

68

November 2014

It was easy for Tammy Shendler, who lived on Indianapolis' far eastside, and Mary Ellen Donat, who lived on the far west side, to see each other once in a while for a cheeseburger at a retro diner halfway between their two homes. They often talked about sharing a ride to Richmond when Tammy made one of her many visits to help her aging adoptive mother. It would give them more than a quick lunch visit. Some day.

They made it happen almost without planning. Tammy emailed one evening that she'd be going to Richmond the next morning to take her mother to the doctor and run other errands for her. Would Mary Ellen like to ride along to see old friends? It'd give them a couple hours to visit on the drive there and back. Plus, Tammy could show Mary Ellen where Ellen had been abandoned.

They met in the parking lot of a Cracker Barrel on the interstate leading to Richmond. It was a cold November morning so Mary Ellen hurriedly slammed the door of her car and rushed to Tammy's. "Whew! Winter is here! I hope it gets warmer by the time we go to Ellen's site."

Tammy turned down the volume on her Sirius radio's contemporary Christian station and leaned over the console to hug her friend hello. "It will be. We're going to have a good time, no matter what. Plus, I guess it wouldn't really be the same if it weren't nasty weather when we go to where Ellen was dumped. That's the only way you'll really get the full effect. Sort of."

The two chatted non-stop as Tammy drove east. An hour into the trip, however, Tammy flipped on the car's turn-signal. "Mind if we get off at Centerville? I'd like to show you the house where your dad found me when I was three years old."

A block off the main intersection of the small town just to the west of Richmond was a white two-story clapboard house. Tammy slowed to a stop near the curb next to the home's back yard. The house was similar to its neighbors, nothing out of the ordinary. Nothing to indicate the horror that it once contained.

"How did they find you?" Mary Ellen asked. "Did neighbors call Dad?"

Tammy hesitated. She started several times to speak, but sighed after each attempt and uttered, "Uh . . . um."

Mary Ellen turned from examining the house and yard to face Tammy with questioning eyes.

"I don't want to offend you."

"You probably won't. I was a little girl and so were you," Mary Ellen assured her.

Tammy's face pleaded. "It's not about us. It's about your dad. My parents hated him. They thought he picked on them because he was always stopping by unannounced and wanting to see us girls."

"That doesn't offend me, Tammy. Dad must've suspected something and he was trying to protect you. What happened the day he finally took you out of the house?"

Tammy related in almost a whisper some of the atrocities that had been visited upon her and her tiny sister by her biological mother and step-father. (Because details are unimaginably unspeakable and personal, it is Tammy's wish that they not be disclosed in this memoir.) She'd been only three years old in 1957, but the trauma of one particular night was indelibly imprinted in the most minute detail into her memory.

"Your dad did drop in a lot. And one night when he came, he knew something was really, really wrong so he came right into our bedroom where Tina and I were in the same crib. I remember him bending down and taking her out. He carried her away and I was crying for her. Calling her name. I can still see him going through the door with my baby sister in his arms."

Wiping tears that softly rolled down her cheeks, Tammy finished, "I found out later, like when I was an adult, that he'd taken her to the hospital. But she was already dead. He came back later with a court order to take me, too."

Mary Ellen could think of nothing to say that would ease the pain beside her. She glanced at the peaceful backyard, lined by fall's neon trees. She remembered the night her father had sat on the edge of her child's bed and told her that sometimes little children are hurt by their own parents. She didn't mention that memory to Tammy. Instead, she said another truth.

"I am not offended. I'm proud of Dad. You may have died, too."

"Yes," Tammy said. "And he was really brave. He had to stand against some pretty powerful men. My biological dad was notorious. We're pretty sure that's why no one was prosecuted in Tina's death. But I was given to welfare to be adopted. He saved me."

"Gosh, and to think you married Ellen's cousin. If not for that, you may never have been her Search Angel.

"It just boggles my mind that you and she had so much in common as babies, had Mary Hart as your adoption advocate, and ended up in the Shendler family. Incredible."

In Richmond, Mary Ellen visited friends while Tammy ran errands for her adoptive mother. Again, they met in the parking lot of a restaurant. This time in Richmond's historic Starr District, just off U.S. 27. When Mary Ellen got into Tammy's car, her friend held up a small brown paper bag. "Three pink ribbons. We'll replace the ones taken from the fence and see how long they last this time."

The women figured it would take only ten or fifteen minutes to reach the site, tie the ribbons and call Ellen in California to share the moment with her. But they drove in circles. Even though the Shendler family home was within a mile of the woods where Ellen was abandoned, and Tammy had visited it many times, she couldn't find it. The autumn sun was by this time masked by trees on the western horizon. Tammy finally placed a call to Ellen.

Following Ellen's verbal directions, they found the spot not far off U.S. 27. Both were surprised it was so close to civilization. The highway perpendicular to the country road was busier now, nearly six decades later, but little else had changed. Mary Ellen could see and feel how remote the woods along the two-lane road was and still is. There was no traffic. And then she saw it: the massive tree her father had talked about, standing sentinel over the spot where Ellen had been dropped.

Appropriately, it had begun to drizzle. The sky was gray, seemingly nonexistent. Clouds of steam dissipated in front of the women's faces as they talked; the chill literally had substance.

With Ellen still on the phone, Tammy and Mary Ellen tied the ribbons to the fence exactly where they'd been placed six months before. Would the land owner take them down? Birds pick away at them to build a nest? Or would the person who'd removed them after the media-covered event be ignorant that the infamous site was once again marked by bright banners?

When Ellen and Mary Ellen visited the lonesome spot six months later, in May of 2015, the three pink ribbons Tammy had bought were still fluttering in the breeze.

69

February 2015

The two had begun to call each other sisters-in-heart. Ellen Suey and Mary Ellen Cordell Donat had become exceptionally close friends over the past year. They texted, emailed or talked daily. The Donats' visit to Riverside in February 2015 sealed the deal. Spending days at the ocean, in Hollywood, hiking, and devouring Bob's homemade eggrolls in the Suey kitchen confirmed that the two were more than mere pen-pals.

"You know," Mary Ellen told the woman who might have been raised her sister, "we've spent almost every minute of the past week together. It could very well have turned out that we didn't like each other after all."

Ellen looked at her in astonishment. It was obvious their relationship surpassed the story and the sheriff. The bond between the two women who could well have been raised together had slowly but progressively strengthened, rooted not only in history but in a love for their Lord and each other.

(Following a September trip to Anaheim to join Ellen at the 2015 Women of Faith Farewell Tour, Mary Ellen was asked by her longtime friend Janet Melling Higgs, "How'd your trip with the baby go?" Puzzled, Corky's daughter asked, "What baby?")

In mid-May 2015, Ellen and Bob would once again be headed to Richmond for another cousin's graduation. The Donats planned to be in the eastern Indiana town to attend the annual Memorial to Fallen Officers at the same time. Ellen and Mary Ellen took advantage of the late winter visit to plan meeting again in the spring.

Neither woman had seen the hunter's grandson in nearly a year. Relationships between the man and the two women had steadily deteriorated over the past several months. The three had agreed following the May 2014 reunion that Mary Ellen Cordell Donat would write a book about the baby found in the woods. The book had been written, copyrighted, and placed with Donat's literary agent, but had not yet been picked up by a publisher.

As they'd gotten to know the hunter's grandson, Ellen and Mary Ellen were grateful that it was not yet God's time to publish. Neither felt comfortable with his account of the story though it may be true. Both Ellen and Mary Ellen know he was definitely there with his grandfather, but neither 1955 newspaper accounts nor the sheriff's memories identify him as the only person who found the abandoned infant after standing atop a fencepost.

Corky, who loved children, never mentioned to his daughter a young teenager; he always referred to the person who found the baby under a tree as "a hunter." The grandson's account of nurses bringing a baby to see him at his junior high school, even though Roseann was in foster care at the time, seems to both women unlikely.

During that February 2015 walk along the beach, they confessed their reservations to one another. Neither remembers who brought it up first.

"I feel bad about writing those things – making up scenarios to fit his story – when my heart tells me I shouldn't have," Mary Ellen told Ellen as they walked arm-in-arm along the shore. "At the time I wrote the book, though, I wanted to believe the fairy tale."

Ellen smiled with understanding. "You and me both. But it wasn't a fairy tale. It was a miracle. There's just one Truth. Let's pray about the book and let God guide us. Meanwhile, can you ask your agent to stop promoting it until we have sure guidance?"

"Yes," Mary Ellen said. "It's got to be God's guidance already that we've both been thinking the same thing without discussing it, and then were prompted to talk about it today."

Mary Ellen and Ellen at the 2015 Women of Faith Farewell Tour in Anaheim, CA

70

May 2017

Beyond plans for several lunches and suppers, a trip to the scene of baby Roseann's appalling abandonment, and lighthearted evenings spent with friends, the Sueys and Donats would attend the annual Memorial to Fallen Officers in May. Mary Ellen had asked Ellen to join her in honoring her father as his name was called during the memorial. The two would walk down the aisle together, hand-in-hand, to lay a flower at the base of a star-shaped flower arrangement. (Following the service each confided to the other that they'd felt his presence; his happiness. Indeed, sisters-in-heart.)

The Sueys flew into the Indianapolis International Airport and met the Donats for breakfast at Cracker Barrel. Eggs and pancakes cooling, Ellen and Mary Ellen talked as their husbands listened and ate their own breakfasts. Later, the two women sat together, gliding lazily back and forth on the Donat's swing on their secluded back deck. Both were being more candid than they'd been in any of their visits or phone calls.

"Ellen, can I ask you about your grandson?"

"Of course."

"I would never have guessed the pain you were in during that reunion last year. I wouldn't guess it now. You're so serene. You're happy, you laugh. I never see you tear up or complain. How do you do it?"

"It's not easy. I do cry. I miss my sweet baby every minute of every day. That first night I wasn't sure I'd ever recover. There were a lot of people praying for my family's peace. I could feel it. And not too many days later, I realized that God had given me a gift when Nin asked me to pick Bubba up from school that week he had half days, just a couple weeks before we lost him. It was rare: to have my man all to myself. Then those three days when we thought he just didn't feel well when I got to take special care of him, those hours were a gift, too.

"I still shed tears for my guy but I know He is in a better place and we will be together one day. He is with his Mudder. I have comfort that can only come from God. He has given me His peace because I also have His promise."

Mary Ellen was quiet. It was a reverent moment.

"I'm going to see Bubba again," Ellen continued. "I'll hold him in my arms again. He's waiting for me. I have assurance of that because Bubba gave his heart to the Lord and Jesus promises that when He comes again, His saints will be with Him."

"You'll see Jesus and Bubba at the same time!"

Ellen nodded. "That's the promise. And that's my comfort. I hope anyone who knows my story – not the one about being left to die as an infant, but the one about losing my first grandchild when he was so young, so active, taken so suddenly – will think about their own eternal life and the indescribable comfort that only God can give in this life.

"My prayer is that anyone who knows that story and sees me living a daily life full of hope and joy will say 'I want that peace, too.' What a blessing to be able to share with others the gift of eternal life through Jesus Christ in such a profound way."

"You are a living testimony," Mary Ellen agreed. "Did Bubba tell you he'd given his heart to Jesus?"

"No. It was Alexander and Alexa. The kids often spent Saturday nights with us then go with us to Harvest Christian Church the next day. Bubba and the other kids participated in children's and Christmas programs. They did a great job.

"But back to how I know with certainty that Bubba is in Heaven: one day after church, when they'd gone home, the three of them went into the bedroom, kneeled, and all three of them asked Jesus into their hearts. Zander told me about it after Bubba died. He talked about it so sweet."

Mary Ellen squeezed Ellen's hand, amazed by her friend's peace within pain.

Ellen smiled broadly. "Bubba was an amazing kid and brought many days of laughter into our lives. Life isn't the same without him but he would want us to keep going and share his love and laughter."

I Thessalonians 4:13-18 – *Brothers and sisters, we do not want you to be uninformed about those who sleep in death, so that you do not grieve like the rest of mankind, who have no hope. For we believe that Jesus died and rose again, and so we believe that God will bring with Jesus those who have fallen asleep in him. According to the Lord's word, we tell you that we who are still alive, who are left until the coming of the Lord, will certainly not precede those who have fallen asleep. For the Lord himself will come down from heaven, with a loud command, with the voice of the archangel and with the trumpet call of God, and the dead in Christ will rise first. After that, we who are still alive and are left will be caught up together with them in the clouds to meet the Lord in the air. And so we will be with the Lord forever. Therefore encourage one another with these words.*

71

"I've contacted Ruby," Corky's daughter told Ellen the night before the Memorial to Fallen Officers. "But I think L.A. convinced her to not talk with you."

Ruby Backmeyer had been one of the three women L.A. had said claimed to suspect the identity of Ellen's biological mother. She was one of the three he'd sent a letter stating erroneous results of the DNA test he'd overseen.

Ellen had hoped that at least one of those women could shed some light on who might have been her biological father as well.

"I think so, too," she said. "I've called and written to the other two women he mentioned and they now say they don't know anything."

There was a brief pause, uncommon when the two were together. It's hard to know what to say when you've been stopped at every turn.

Mary Ellen told Ellen as they discussed the next day's visit, "Ruby was a good friend of Mom and Dad's, and I always liked her. I haven't seen her since Mom died. I told her truthfully on the phone today that I'd like to see her before Tom and I move to New Mexico. When I told her you'd be with me, she said 'okay' but that she didn't want to talk about anything to do with your history."

"Okay. I won't ask any questions. We'll just visit and maybe there'll be a miracle."

The blooming Indiana trees were just past their prime, but still beautifully flowering, when Mary Ellen parked outside Ruby's condo on Richmond's east side a couple hours before the Memorial.

"Ready?" Mary Ellen asked.

Ellen opened the car door. "I won't ask a thing. I promise."

Ruby, a small woman in her eighties stylishly dressed as if she were meeting friends for a luncheon, greeted the women at her door. She welcomed them inside with a hug for her old friends' daughter and a genuine smile and handshake for Ellen.

Ellen, still hoping for a miracle but honoring Ruby's wish for no questions, walked across the bright living room to sit on an exquisite heirloom wing-backed chair. She smiled, taking in the neat room with its antiques and artwork. She'd barely settled into her seat when she got her miracle.

"You look just like your mother," Ruby said as if in wonderment.

Ellen and Mary Ellen were surprised. They'd hoped for this moment, and felt that Ruby may decide to tell Ellen something after getting to know her. But this was so unexpected and sudden that neither woman said anything in response to Ruby's pronouncement.

Both were soon sorry they hadn't replied because Ruby immediately asked if they'd like something to drink. The younger women shook their heads. Ruby then began a conversation about friends and family familiar to both her and the Cordells' daughter. As they chatted, Ellen sat smiling politely. She seemed to be patiently waiting for a return to the subject of her biological parentage. In reality, she was thinking she may need a Band-Aid if she continued to bite her tongue much longer.

Then just as suddenly as she'd noted the similarity in Ellen's appearance and the woman with whom she'd worked at Wayne Works decades earlier, Ruby said, "I have so many good memories of your mother."

She was animated as she told Ellen about her biological mother's job at the Wayne Works, her friendliness, and her penchant for fun. Ruby laughed recalling a few stories about the men and dates the woman would entertain co-workers with on Monday mornings. She continued by recalling for Ellen a get-together co-workers had after they'd retired. Several former Wayne Works secretaries had met for lunch at MCL Cafeteria not far from Ruby's present home.

"A lot of time had passed since we'd been young," Ruby said about that lunch. "I guess your mother felt safe to confess a secret she'd been keeping."

Ruby's small audience held their breaths. Would this be the information Ellen had been waiting to hear? Would she at last know the circumstances of her abandonment and even who so heartlessly dropped her over that barbed wire fence then callously drove away?

"She told us," Ruby said, as if she were about to repeat an innocent tale that had at one time been scandalous but now was merely a harmless memory, "she'd had a baby when she was very young. It was a little boy. She'd been able to keep her pregnancy a secret and gave the boy up for adoption."

Ellen exhaled. She'd heard this information before. She felt, though, that the visit with her biological mother's former co-worker was worthwhile. Though she hadn't heard any clues that might lead her to her biological father, Ruby had confirmed the identity of her biological mother and that she was known to be able to conceal a pregnancy.

(Note to readers: Ellen has promised her biological aunt and cousins that she will protect their identities by not divulging the name of the woman who gave her birth.)

Mary Ellen glanced at the Seth Thomas clock above Ellen's chair. She stood from her seat on the sofa. "I've so much enjoyed our visit, Ruby. We have to be going, though. The Memorial to Fallen Officers is going to start in about an hour. By the time we get down to the city building . . . "

"I may have a name for you," Ruby interrupted, looking at Ellen, who'd half risen from her seat. "Someone who might be your father."

Both Ellen and Mary Ellen sat again.

Ruby continued, "There was a supervisor at Wayne Works. He was married, but he and your mother had an affair. I remember he used to come into the office quite often to see her. I can give you his name, but I have no idea where he is now, or even if he's still alive."

Sitting on the edge of her flowered chair, Ruby revealed the man's name then pressed her mouth into an expectant smile as if indicating she had nothing more to say. The young women waited, but she had indeed finished speaking. Mary Ellen rose and Ellen followed. Ruby walked them to her door. She thanked them for the visit and said how much she enjoyed seeing Mary Ellen again, reiterating her love for the girl's parents, then warmly embraced Ellen.

"I am so thrilled to have met you," she told her former co-worker's biological daughter. "You are a lovely woman."

Barely six months following the visit, Ruby suddenly but peacefully passed away.

Unfortunately, neither the City Directory nor the telephone directory for 1955 has notations for the man whose name Ellen carried away with her from Ruby Backmeyer.

72

2015 - 2017

The Sueys and Donats spent another few days together in May of 2015 before Ellen and Bob flew home to Riverside. Within a month the Donats moved to Santa Fe, New Mexico. By fall of 2015, the women and the hunter's grandson mutually agreed to legally terminate their book agreement. While Ellen and Mary Ellen continue to enjoy their friendship, neither has communicated with the hunter's grandson since.

In the autumn of 2016 the Sueys invited the Donats to accompany them on a vacation to their condominium in Kauai, Hawaii. Just as she'd thrilled Bubba with a trip to LAX in a limousine, Ellen arranged for a similar VIP experience for her sister-in-heart.

The following spring, Ellen and Bob brought along Debra and several other friends on a Royal Caribbean book club cruise to the Bahamas with the Donats. The book to be discussed was Mary Ellen's first novel, *In the Shadow of Her Hat*. During the cruise, with enthusiastic encouragement from other book club travelers, they decided that it was time to tell Ellen's story.

Neither woman is sure why they feel it's in God's perfect timing to publish this memoir while two important pieces to Ellen's puzzle are yet to be found. As of fall 2017, Ellen's biological father is still unknown, as is the person who meant for her to die that cold and wet autumn sixty-two years ago.

It is their hope that Ellen's miraculous story, one that proves life isn't a fairy tale or that followers of Christ aren't exempt from heartbreak or hardship, will result in readers finding joy in the Lord and in His love.

Tom and Mary Ellen Donat with
Ellen and Bob Suey in Kauai, Hawaii, 2016
(Mary Ellen is wearing the lei Ellen presented
her upon arrival in the Islands)

Mary Ellen's grandchildren with the Sueys in their kitchen, November 2017

Afterword

December 2017

During their search for the missing identities of Ellen's biological father and the person who abandoned her, the women have tapped the memories and expertise of dozens of people.

Even Mary Ellen's friends, former State Senator Allen Paul, current Wayne County Sheriff Jeff Cappa, and Indiana State Excise Director Matt Strittmatter, were unable to find or have opened government files or records of the tiny baby found in Wayne County woods in 1955.

Incredibly, Reid Memorial Hospital patient and personnel files were reportedly lost in a flood, there are no sheriff files on the case, and no Indiana State Police evidence records of it. Perhaps lost information could have been found in adoption attorney John Harlan's files, Reid Memorial Hospital records, files that have disappeared from the departments of Wayne County Welfare, the Wayne County Sheriff's Department and the Indiana State Police Laboratory.

Loss of one or two files may be explainable or understandable. More than once Ellen and Mary Ellen have lamented to one another, "How could so many records be missing?"

Perhaps it's true that Ellen's biological father, or the person who meant for her to die as an infant under a tree near a barbed wire fence, was indeed someone influential and powerful.

Ellen has learned that citing the Freedom of Information Act has no effect when files are missing or destroyed. In her case, that covers every single file and record except one. Wayne County Superior Court 1 adoption records are sealed. At the publishing of this memoir, Ellen is pursuing a court order that may open her adoption record.

She continues to search, following up on information she receives from time to time from people who have heard about her and think they may know who her biological father could be.

It is very possible that someone still living knows his identity. That same person may know who dropped Ellen over the barbed wire fence that cold, wet autumn night. They may know the reason why.

He or she may be that very person.

Hope remains that someone will come forward with solid information or a confession. Ellen is not interested in pursuing legal retribution. She is grateful that God spared her life, placed her in a Christian home with loving parents, and has, in His perfect time, revealed to her all she needs to know at this moment. She is confident that some bright day He will provide the rest of her story.

Her faith is unwavering.

Hebrews 13:6 – *So we can say with confidence, "The LORD is my helper, so I will have no fear. What can mere people do to me?"*

My story is such an inspiration of God's love, grace and mercy.

God has showed me and many others how He can take a horrible situation and make it beautiful. God brought me full circle. He blessed me with loving parents growing up. Then 58 years later I got to meet my biological aunt and two cousins. They have embraced me as family.

There is hope in the bleak moments. God does things for a reason and we don't always understand but we need to trust Him.

Ellen Suey

Mary Ellen Cordell Donat and Mary Ellen Test Suey
in Riverside, CA (2015)

Made in the USA
San Bernardino, CA
29 May 2018